Wind in the Rigging

Wind in the Rigging

A Study of Acts 9—12 and Its Meaning for Today

by

Randal Earl Denny

Beacon Hill Press of Kansas City
Kansas City, Missouri

Cover Art: Crandall Vail

Permission to quote from the following copyrighted versions of the
Bible is acknowledged with appreciation:

The Holy Bible, New International Version (NIV), copyright © 1978 by
the New York International Bible Society.

The *New Testament in Modern English* (Phillips), Revised Edition © J.
B. Phillips, 1958, 1960, 1972. By permission of the Macmillan
Publishing Co.

The Living Bible (TLB), © 1971 by Tyndale House Publishers, Wheaton,
Ill.

Unless otherwise indicated, all scriptures are taken from the NIV.

10 9 8 7 6 5 4 3 2 1

Dedication

To my four district superintendents:
Leaders with a heart
Tender enough to feel my hurts
Human enough to laugh with me
Good men in whom there is no guile
E. L. Cornelison
W. H. Deitz
Paul Benefiel
Walter Lanman

Contents

Foreword 9

Preface 11

Acknowledgments 12

1 Arrested by Jesus *(Acts 9:1-9)* 13

2 Armed with Love *(Acts 9:10-19)* 23

3 Make Use of Your Failure *(Acts 9:19-30)* 34

4 ". . . and All Is Well!" *(Acts 9:31-43)* 46

5 "At Your Service, Lord!" *(Acts 10:1-23)* 56

6 "Fill My Cup, Lord!" *(Acts 10:23-48)* 68

7 Baptized with the Spirit—Equipped to Serve
(Acts 11:1-18) 78

8 Are You Christlike? *(Acts 11:19-30)* 87

9 Specializing in the Impossible *(Acts 12:1-19)* 97

Notes 111

Bibliography 113

Foreword

To be able to communicate on paper as well as in person is a rare gift. Evidence of this fact is the very few sermons that actually make it into print. Publishers know the market is limited, often restricted to only a group of ministers who are in want of preaching material.

But Randal Denny's writings are different. Ever since his first book was published I have looked forward to further ones. As a preacher I have found his printed sermons filled with ideas and starters for sermons of my own. Beyond being a preacher, I find his writings fresh, insightful, sometimes witty, and always applicable.

The reading of this manuscript met all my expectations. This time the work of the Holy Spirit in the New Testament Church comes alive as one recognizes the same could happen in today's church. The miracles, the answers to prayer, the unusual deliverances are not relegated to past history, but the "wind in the rigging" is setting the course, directing the church, and empowering those who have been filled yet today. We owe this successful pastor-author a deep debt of gratitude for this clear stimulus to our faith.

—JERALD D. JOHNSON

Preface

The halyard slapping against a flagpole, the flapping, snapping sounds of a flag in a brisk breeze often go unheeded by people passing by. But not I, and others like me, to whom the sounds conjure up mental and emotional pictures of a boat under sail. There's an indescribable, zestful song in our ear listening to wind in the rigging.

To one sitting in a sailboat becalmed, powerless, directionless, emotionless, looking for a distant breeze, unable to make progress, wind in the rigging is pure music—the sweet sound of power, of progress, of joy! It's as if the sailboat comes alive as wind sings through the rigging! Any wind is better than none.

When the church sits becalmed in placid seas of social conformity, there's a longing in the heart for a fresh, new breeze of the Holy Spirit. As God's wind of the Spirit moves through the rigging of Old Ship Zion, a contagion of enthusiasm begins to spread, excitement lights the watchful eye, life itself quickens, hope stirs. Hoisting the sails of faith, we catch the Spirit's freshening touch!

Luke, in Acts 9—12, describes the moving of the Holy Spirit empowering and directing His Church. No more coasting along narrow shorelines of Judaism. The Spirit's wind in the rigging finds the Church on the "broad reach," sailing horizons of the world under the ensign of the Cross.

There's a longing in my heart for the breath of God to sweep through with a fresh, new breeze in our day. While studying these pages in Acts, let's listen for the song of wind in the rigging once again!

11

Acknowledgments

The Kahului Church of the Nazarene on the beautiful Hawaiian island of Maui provided the opportunity to write this manuscript. Pastor Herb Kamada took his vacation elsewhere and allowed my wife and me to use his parsonage, his car, his pulpit on Sundays—and his ocean and beaches the remainder of the week. Later, preaching through Acts 9—12 in my own pastorate, Spokane Valley Church, I was able to revise and put on the finishing touches. I wish to thank both churches for making this possible.

Appreciation is hereby expressed for permission to quote from copyrighted material as follows:

Abingdon Press: George Arthur Buttrick, ed., *The Interpreter's Bible*, vol. 9.

Beacon Hill Press of Kansas City: John T. Seamands, *On Tiptoe with Love.*

Harper and Brothers: Clovis G. Chappell, *Men That Count.*

Regal Books: Jerry Cook, *Love, Acceptance, and Forgiveness.*

Vision House Publishers: Ray C. Stedman, *Birth of the Body.*

Westminster Press: William Barclay, *The Acts of the Apostles, The Daily Study Bible.*

Zondervan Publishing House: W. A. Criswell, *Filling and Gifts of the Holy Spirit;* Haralan Popov, *Tortured for His Faith.*

I owe a great debt to Chauncey Middleton who made our trip to Hawaii possible—providing passage, fellowship, and the solitude I needed for writing. Friends like that are a gift from God.

RANDAL EARL DENNY
Spokane Valley Church
Spokane, Wash.

CHAPTER 1

Arrested by Jesus

Acts 9:1-9

Luke has an interesting way of introducing main characters in the drama of the Book of Acts. Before the spotlight beams down on a leading character, Luke first shows him in the background of the previous act. Barnabas was just a face in the crowd before coming to the fore. Stephen and Philip were names on the ballot for deacons—and then Luke moves them onto center stage. Young Saul stood on the edge of the circle holding the coats of those stoning Stephen. Suddenly, in Acts 9, Saul is engulfed in the spotlight—and we can never forget him.

In Saul's frenzied flight to Damascus to arrest followers of Jesus, he is dramatically arrested—by Jesus himself! And Saul is forever a prisoner of Christ.

Saul was such a fanatic, Christ struck him down on the Damascus Road. He had to get Saul's attention. As William McCumber put it, "Cooling down a fanatic is easier than warming up a corpse!"

Luke devoted about 8 percent of the Book of Acts to the story of Paul's conversion, including three separate accounts—more than any other subject in Acts. Two-thirds of Acts describes Paul's part in the development of the Early Church.

As an author, Paul wrote at least 13 of the 27 New Testament books. He carried the gospel into Asia Minor, Greece, and Rome. He personally confronted the forces that would have split the Early Church.

Saul was a native of Tarsus, a major commercial center in what is known today as Turkey. Born a Jew in a Greek-speaking city, Saul was multilingual and multicultural. After studying at the renowned University of Tarsus, Saul continued his education in Jerusalem under Gamaliel. Later Paul wrote, "Under Gamaliel I was thoroughly trained in the law of our fathers" (Acts 22:3).

Paul possessed the logical mind of a philosopher, the spiritual insight of a theologian, and the practical skills of an organizer. With his entrance into the Christian faith, it could no longer be said that Christians were ignorant and unlettered men! We owe him a great debt.

Arrested by Jesus, Saul had a dramatic conversion—yet the basic steps are universal.

Saul Began Convinced of His Own Moral Goodness

Saul was sincere. "Meanwhile, Saul was still breathing out murderous threats against the Lord's disciples" (v. 1). Later he describes his sincerity: "as for zeal, persecuting the church; as for legalistic righteousness, faultless" (Phil. 3:6). But he was wrong.

Our beliefs must be true as well as sincere. Dr. W. T. Purkiser often quoted these lines:

> Consider the case of poor Will.
> Poor Willy is with us no more.
> What Willy thought was H_2O
> Was really H_2SO_4. (Sulfuric acid)

Though hurting people, Saul believed himself to be in good standing with God. And many people go through the motions of religion sincere but wrong. As one noted, "They have been brought up in the church; they have heard the prayers all their lives; they have seen the bread broken at the altar, but they have never known. Like a man who sees another man swim, understands the principle of it, and could himself go through all the motions, yet who never dares surrender himself to the buoyancy of the water. These people see the whole thing in principle but never feel the everlasting arms underneath them."[1]

Charlie Brown dragged his baseball bat and mitt. In dismay he talks to himself: "Good grief! One hundred and eighty-four to nothing! I don't understand it—how can we lose when we're so sincere?"

Charles C. Ryrie adds: "If sincerity alone could get you to heaven, then why does the Bible say: 'Believe on the Lord Jesus Christ, and thou shalt be saved'? (Acts 16:31, KJV). Why did Jesus Christ himself say: 'No man cometh unto the Father, but by me'? (John 14:6, KJV). Sincerity can't pay the penalty for sin but Jesus Christ did. Sincerity can't give you the gift of eternal life, but Jesus Christ will—IF you will trust Him to be your Saviour."[2]

Saul was intense. He hated what he thought was wrong: "Saul was still breathing out murderous threats" (v. 1). The Greek word for "still" suggests an attitude held in spite of something. Here's a little clue: Saul continued to hate intensely—in spite of something going on inside of him. Arnold Airhart commented, "There was a strange fury in his actions, the kind of thing that drives a man who is losing his inner confidence."[3] Blind loyalty spurred Saul from house to house seeking out victims for punishment.

Eric Hoffer, in his book *The Passionate State of Mind*, noted: "The remarkable thing is that we . . . hate others when we hate ourselves. We are tolerant toward others when we tolerate ourselves. We forgive others when we forgive ourselves. It is not love of self but hatred of self which is at the root of the troubles that afflict our world."

Saul was insecure. He craved advancement—at the cost of hurting people in the process. Being insecure, Saul was obsessed with recognition, having become a powerful leader at such a young age in a Jewish society governed by elders. Pride masks insecurity!

One trombonist repeatedly claimed to be the greatest in the world. Someone challenged him to prove it. "I don't have to prove it," he replied. "I admit it!"

That insecurity is a warning flag—something is wrong inside Saul.

Saul Becomes Convicted of His Own Sins

According to 1 Maccabees 15:15, the Roman government gave the Jewish high priest permission to extradite any Jewish violator of religious law back to Jerusalem. Going to Caiaphas the high priest, Saul received legal papers to arrest the Jewish people who had fled from Jerusalem after the murder of Stephen.

Saul set his sights on Damascus—a refuge for many followers of Jesus. One of the oldest cities of the world still occupied today, Damascus lies 70 miles inland from the Mediterranean Sea and 200 miles north of Jerusalem—a six-day journey. That gave Saul a lot of time to think—and think—and think.

The reflection of Jesus chafed inside him. Probably Saul had never seen Jesus—but he had seen Him reflected in the lives of His followers. The contrast created a deep inner struggle. His Christian victims evidenced a peace and victory denied him in his religion by works.

The memory of Stephen haunted him. Saul had watched him die—and as he was dying Stephen asked for forgiveness for his tormentors. The shouting of the mob, the uplifted face shining with heaven's glory, and the words of that last prayer, "Lord, do not hold this sin against them" (Acts 7:60), made an indelible impression on Saul. Augustine was right: "If Stephen had not prayed, the Church would not have had Paul."

Saul's conversion was no sudden surprise; in his heart there had been a prelude. It was like Stanley said of David Livingstone, "He made me a Christian, and he never knew he was doing it!" The lives of real Christians are but mirrors to reflect the glory of God. A mirror never calls attention to itself unless it has flaws in it.

The light of Jesus came upon Saul. Determined to get to Damascus, Saul kept traveling at midday—the time people normally rested from the heat. Outside the borders of Palestine, Saul was arrested by Jesus! "As he neared Damascus on his journey, suddenly a light from heaven flashed around him" (v. 3). The floodgates of heaven opened and the glory of God splashed all around. Whose sin can remain hidden in the presence of Jesus?

Later Paul described his experience to King Agrippa: "About noon, O king, as I was on the road, I saw a light from heaven, brighter than the sun, blazing around me and my companions" (Acts 26:13). The glory of Jesus caught Saul's attention. The "light from heaven" symbolized the great revelation about to flood Saul's life. In that awesome moment, Saul "fell to the ground" (v. 4), a natural reaction to a heavenly visitation.

Charles Lamb emphasized Jesus' superiority: "What would we do if Shakespeare came into the room? We would rise to our feet. But what would we do if Jesus came into this room? We would all fall on our knees!"

The glory of Jesus' presence reveals our unworthiness: "Search me, O God, and know my heart; test me and know my anxious thoughts. See if there is any offensive way in me" (Ps. 139:23-24).

The voice of Jesus called to Saul. "He . . . heard a voice

17

say to him, 'Saul, Saul, why do you persecute me?'" (v. 4). In answering that question, Saul had to make an important discovery of himself. One cannot walk with God without discovering himself.

It was as though Jesus were saying, "Why do you think you can stop Me, Saul? You can't undo My great work! Why are you driven like this?" Jesus is the march of God through human history—and Saul thought he could stamp it out forever!

In John Masefield's book *The Trial of Jesus*, Pilate's wife asked the centurion who announced Jesus' death, "Do you think He is dead?"

The Roman centurion replied, "No, lady, I don't."

"Then where is He?"

"Loose in the world, lady, where neither Roman nor Jew can stop His truth!"

We cannot stop Him either—by force, by neglect, or by lip service. Our doubts neither make Him cease to exist nor delay His imminent second coming!

Saul cried out, "Who are you, Lord?" (v. 5).

Jesus showed Saul his sin: "I am Jesus, whom you are persecuting" (v. 5). By birth, training, and habit, Saul viewed religion as obedience to prescribed laws and rules. Therefore, Saul had a preconceived idea of Jesus as a moral anarchist. His preconceptions blinded him to the beauty of Jesus. This unexpected revelation of a risen Christ made Saul see his terrible sins. He had been wrong: Jesus is the Christ—alive and well! The captor became captive to Jesus.

It comes as a solemn warning—if one deliberately hurts God's children, he is hurting Jesus Christ. Jesus identifies with His people.

At the moment Saul felt the powerful conviction for his sin and guilt, Jesus' words kept ringing in his mind: "Saul, Saul . . ." (v. 4). There's a familiar echo in the repetition. Hearing of the death of his rebellious son, King David cried out

18

with a broken heart: "O my son Absalom! O Absalom, my son, my son!" (2 Sam. 19:4).

Centuries later, a descendant of David looked over the city of His rebellious people and cried with a broken heart: "O Jerusalem, Jerusalem . . . how often I have longed to gather your children together, as a hen gathers her chicks under her wings, but you were not willing" (Matt. 23:37).

And now the risen Christ calls with a broken heart to the young rebel: "Saul, Saul . . ." It is not the cry of anger but the cry of love for a wayward man. Jesus expresses profound compassion. That's how He calls each one today!

Saul Was Converted from His Own Lonely Way

The zealous Jew was captivated by Christ. Later he wrote about being arrested by Jesus: "What a wretched man I am! Who will rescue me from this body of death? Thanks be to God—through Jesus Christ our Lord! . . . Therefore, there is now no condemnation for those who are in Christ Jesus, because through Christ Jesus the law of the Spirit of life set me free from the law of sin and death" (Rom. 7:24—8:2).

Immediately Saul trusted Christ. His conversion was complete. His trust in Jesus evoked a threefold response.

First, Saul admitted his need for Christ: "What wilt thou have me to do?" (v. 6, KJV). When one is born again, he knows there's a dividing line—a "before" and "after." "Before" there's a gnawing sense of guilt; "after" there's the joy found in Christ.

One man testified, "I never saw Jesus until I saw Him through my sins." He was then brought face-to-face with his need for Jesus.

The Master makes available a new chapter, a new beginning. The moral leopard can change his spots—at the foot of the Cross. One begins by admitting his need for the Savior.

Second, Saul acknowledged Jesus as Lord. After Jesus identified himself, Saul called out, "Lord!" More than a title of respect, it was the surrender of his life to the Lordship of Jesus. And Paul testifies to it many times in his sermons and letters.

Christ stands ready to occupy the center of one's inner life. One must first acknowledge Him as Savior and Lord.

Third, Saul announced his availability: "Lord, what wilt thou have me to do?" That's the spirit of total surrender! Giving God our availability opens the new life for directions from the new Commander in Chief.

Richard Baxter's last words typified his saintly life: "Lord, what You will, where You will, and when You will." That's the picture of the truly converted heart.

One writer put it clearly: "Many Christian lives are unproductive because Christians sometimes fail for years to ask God, What will You have me to do? Saul asked for instructions *immediately* upon his conversion. Some believers *never* get around to asking.

"How about *you*? Do you *know* what God wants you to be doing? Are you *doing* it?"[4]

Saul also obeyed Christ. Jesus gave Saul instructions: "Now get up and go into the city, and you will be told what you must do" (v. 6). It is the familiar theme, "Trust and Obey."

First, Jesus said, "Get up. Get up out of the dust. You are a child of God now. Quit crawling around in the dirt of guilt and remorse and self-incrimination. Dust yourself off—and leave it all behind!"

Second, "Go into the city." That was more difficult than it seems at first glance: "Saul got up from the ground, but when he opened his eyes he could see nothing. So they led him by the hand into Damascus" (v. 8). A man named Judas in Damascus was prepared to host an ambassador of the high priest, but Saul entered Damascus differently than planned. He arrived blind, afflicted, humbled—"led . . . by the hand." He was now a prisoner of Jesus Christ.

Immediately Saul had to learn dependence. Learning the

lessons of dependency of spirit is a prelude to God's great work in us and through us.

Third, Jesus said, "You will be told what you must do." "Go to Damascus and wait. Have patience. 'Be still, and know that I am God' [Ps. 46:10]. Learn to trust—even when you don't see. Take one step at a time." The old hymn expresses the idea beautifully:

> Lead, kindly Light, amid th'encircling gloom;
> Lead Thou me on!
> The night is dark, and I am far from home;
> Lead Thou me on!
> Keep Thou my feet; I do not ask to see
> The distant scene; one step enough for me.

Saul patiently obeyed Jesus' commands without argument or complaint: "For three days he was blind, and did not eat or drink anything" (v. 9). How reminiscent of Jonah's three-day seminar—in darkness without food or drink. In each case, it was a time of turning around the direction of life.

For three days in the tomb of imposed darkness, Saul did a lot of thinking—especially rethinking! He had completed a U-turn, a reversal of mental attitude and life's direction. In Acts 9:10-19, we learn that Saul prayed a great deal seeking to bring his mind into harmony with his life-shaking experience. He was discovering, "But whatever was to my profit I now consider loss for the sake of Christ" (Phil. 3:7).

As one begins to follow Jesus, He imparts a whole new value system. One does not spring into completed maturity but enters God's kingdom ready for a pilgrimage of faith. One is not ready-made but ready to be made in the likeness of Christ. Each person should ask himself: "Where am I in my pilgrimage? Am I convinced of my moral failure? Am I convicted of my personal sins? Or am I now forgiven and now possessing new life in Christ?"

Lyttleton and West, two British lawyers, were convinced

21

Christianity was a hoax founded on two false experiences: the resurrection of Christ and the conversion of Paul. They agreed to join together to disprove these two so-called miraculous events. They decided, "Destroy them and Christianity would die!"

After dividing the assignment, the two men went through long, painstaking research. Finally they met to discuss their findings. West asked Lyttleton, "What are the results of your study?"

With great feeling, Lyttleton replied, "I have studied the conversion of Paul. I have investigated every argument and supposed solution in order to explain it away. I have rejected them all. I have accepted the Christ of Paul—I am a Christian now."

Turning to West, he asked, "And what are the results of your studies?"

West answered, "I have investigated every argument presented against the resurrection of Jesus Christ. I have concluded it is the best-attested fact of all history. I, too, have accepted Christ and I'm a Christian!"

Paul wrote for all to know, "I am not ashamed of the gospel, because it is the power of God for the salvation of everyone who believes" (Rom. 1:16).

It's not how dramatic your encounter with Jesus but how decisive your response!

CHAPTER 2

Armed with Love

Acts 9:10-19

During the American Civil War, President Lincoln made some kind remarks toward the Confederates. One woman asked how he could say such nice things about enemies he should be trying to destroy.

"Madam," he replied, "do I not destroy them when I ✓ make them my friends?"

There are many ways to fight. Some fight with fists, but it never proves who is right—only who is stronger. Some fight with words and win arguments, but it doesn't prove who is right—only who is more adept with words or who has the loudest voice.

There is a way to win: Be armed with love. Only strong men can fight with love. Weaklings use fists—or arguments—or guns. But those are no match for love. Dr. Ralph Earle put it, "It is natural to love one's friends; it is supernatural to love one's enemies."[1]

Festo Kivengere, bishop of Uganda, said: "One day I opened my poor heart to Jesus Christ, and the cross did a miracle. God set me free, sending me through the fields to ask people's forgiveness. I remember the day I bicycled fifty miles to a white man whom I had hated. I stood there in his house, telling him what Christ had done for me, and that now I was free and saw him as my brother. English as he was, he stood there weeping. We were in each other's arms. I used no weapon, but Christ's love had won. This is victory! This is the power which the world is desperately in need of."[2]

The Lord sent Ananias, armed only with love, to Saul. Saul had been blinded, stunned by his sins in the presence of Jesus. Broken, drained of arrogance, Saul needed someone to bring healing, to explain and give assurance. Ananias obediently went to disciple the new convert. Every young convert needs the help of older Christians. Then, as now, God calls the mature Christian to minister to a babe in Christ. Neither knowledge nor eloquence steadies the young, grasping mind; only love can do that.

Ananias held no official position in the church. Though neither apostle nor bishop, he was available, armed with love: "a devout observer of the law and highly respected by all the Jews living there. He stood beside me" (Acts 22:12-13), testifies Paul. Ananias demonstrates for us the role of a discipler.

Love Kept Ananias Tuned In to God's Voice

Love creates a climate for communication—human or divine. "In Damascus there was a disciple named Ananias. The Lord called to him in a vision, 'Ananias!'

"'Yes, Lord,' he answered" (v. 10).

Because Ananias loved God, it was easy for him to hear Christ's call. His openness enabled him to be tuned in to whatever the Lord might say. The Master simply called out, "Ananias!"—his name meaning, "The Lord is gracious." God, in His grace, needed Ananias to assist Saul. With perfect timing God picked a man who was sensitive and receptive.

Ananias was attentive to God. The Lord says, "I will guide thee with mine eye" (Ps. 32:8, KJV). Most people have seen a person direct a child or spouse to do something with-

24

out saying a word. Even in a room full of people, the attention is caught. By a slight movement of the eyes some direction is signaled. Only the attentive one caught it.

God can direct us if we are attentive for His direction. We must be in tune with Him. Isaiah said, "The Lord will guide you always" (Isa. 58:11).

Because Ananias loved God, it was easy for him to be responsive. There was an immediate "Yes, Lord." His response was like answering the telephone, "Ananias here!" He was available, ready for orders. That's the response of love: "Yes, Lord."

A 12-year-old boy came in from a long day working in the hayfields. He was tired, dirty, and hungry. His father, rather hesitatingly, requested, "Jim, I wish you would take this package to the village for me."

His first impulse was to refuse—but he knew his aging father would have to go. Jim agreed.

"Thank you, Jim," the old man added. "I was going myself, but I don't feel very strong today."

As the boy started out on foot, his father walked with him to the road leading to town two miles away. As they parted, the father put his hand on the boy's shoulder, saying again, "Thank you, my son. You've always been a good boy to me, Jim."

The lad hurried to town and back. As he came near the house, a crowd of farmhands surrounded the door. One of them approached him with tears: "Your father fell dead just as he reached the house. The last words he ever spoke were to you."

That boy became a doctor and later reminisced: "I'm an old man now, but I have thanked God over and over again through all these years that Father's last words were, 'You've always been a good boy to me.'"

Jesus desires that kind of obedient love from us—as He

did from Ananias. Jesus says, "If anyone loves me, he will obey" (John 14:23).

Love Made Ananias Receptive to God's Instructions

Ananias understood exactly what Christ was asking: "The Lord told him, 'Go to the house of Judas on Straight Street and ask for a man from Tarsus named Saul, for he is praying. In a vision he has seen a man named Ananias come and place his hands on him to restore his sight'" (vv. 11-12).

God knows the exact address of His children. "The house of Judas on Straight Street." Judas, the Jewish host, expecting the ambassador of the high priest, surprisingly entertained the ambassador of Jesus! Straight Street is still today one of the main east-west streets through Damascus. And the Lord knew right where it was.

The Lord described Saul to Ananias: "a man from Tarsus named Saul, for he is praying." Saul spent those three sightless days in prayer. Though he had been saying prayers all his life, he had met the living Christ face-to-face. As Saul prayed out of desperation, God was preparing for him.

Saul would need the tender care of a man like Ananias who had known the Lord for years and had learned to pray and trust God. Meanwhile the Lord was making preparation in the hearts of both Saul and Ananias. Three persons were involved in that incident of prayer: the man who prayed, the God who heard, and the man through whom the answer came. And Ananias understood himself to be the Ananias God had revealed to Saul in the vision.

Ananias knew it involved great risk: "'Lord,' Ananias answered, 'I have heard many reports about this man and all the harm he has done to your saints in Jerusalem. And he has come here with authority from the chief priests to arrest all who call on your name'" (vv. 13-14).

"But, Lord," Ananias responded. Jesus has just given him

an incredible assignment: "Go and lay hands on Public En- ✓
emy Number One." To admit being a follower of Jesus had
been like signing one's own death warrant. Discipleship
means risk. Ananias was armed with love—and love always
takes the risk of being hurt. Obedience to God's will may cost
much—but not as much as ignoring God's will.

Ananias hesitated—not in rebellion, but to ask for more
understanding. He did not oppose God's plan, but he did
want to be sure he heard correctly—a plea for clarification. It ✓
isn't sinful to question God with a desire to more fully know
and follow His will. There is a difference between unbelief
and questioning. Unbelief is spiritual rebellion—looking for a
way to avoid God's will. Questioning is seeking God's perfect
will, committed to obedience as it is understood.

There's no rebellion in Ananias' comments. He just
wanted to be sure the Lord knew all the facts about the risks
involved with Saul.

Ananias was willing to see Saul from God's point of
view. "But the Lord said to Ananias, 'Go! This man is my
chosen instrument to carry my name before the Gentiles and
their kings and before the people of Israel. I will show him
how much he must suffer for my name'" (vv. 15-16).

How did God view Saul? "My chosen instrument" or "He ✓
is a chosen vessel unto me" (KJV). What a description of
Christian witness! A vessel is not important of itself but is
valuable for what it contains. A milk carton has little value
without milk; yet without a container milk would be lost. If
milk is to give nourishment, it must be put in some kind of
milk carton.

God carefully selected Saul for a particular assignment.
Saul, the chosen vessel, was not much in himself but became
useful in spite of imperfections: "But we have this treasure in
jars of clay to show that this all-surpassing power is from
God and not from us" (2 Cor. 4:7). One has noted, "It is not

27

the vessel that counts, but the precious contents which it holds!"[3]

Ananias began to see, not what Saul had been, but what God would make of him. Who among us wishes to drag his unchristian past around with him? Of all people, the church must be redemptive—forgetting the past, accepting people as they are, viewing them as God does: useful vessels of God's love, saved to serve—in spite of themselves. Since Jesus selected Saul and loved him, Ananias would not reject him.

Prayer changes people. God works on our attitudes until we begin to see through His eyes the very people we have feared or faulted or forsaken. We must learn to see each one as a person of infinite worth. That's how God sees each one of us.

Ananias trusted God in spite of the risk. "Then Ananias went" (v. 17). Kirsopp Lake defined this kind of trust: "Faith is not belief in spite of evidence but life in scorn of consequence!" When Ananias left the safety of his own house, he demonstrated a deep trust in God. He was saying with his life what he had said with his lips, "Yes, Lord!"

A missionary friend of mine jotted down six words in the flyleaf of his Bible which typifies Ananias: "No reservations; no regrets; no retreat." Jeremy Taylor once said, "It is impossible for that man to despair who remembers that his Helper is omnipotent." God doesn't lift us out of the battles of life, but He keeps us steady during the struggles! A. M. Overton expressed it well:

> My Father's way may twist and turn,
>   My heart may throb and ache;
> But in my soul I'm glad I know
>   He maketh no mistake.
>
> My cherished plans may go astray,
>   My hopes may fade away;

28

But still I'll trust my Lord to lead,
For He doth know the way.

Though night be dark and it may seem
That day will never break,
I'll pin my faith, my all in Him;
He maketh no mistake.

There's so much now I cannot see,
My eyesight's far too dim;
But come what may, I'll simply trust
And leave it all to Him.

For by and by the mists will lift,
And plain it all He'll make.
Through all the way, though dark to me,
He made not one mistake.

Love Empowered Ananias to Be Obedient to God's Call

Armed with love, Ananias obeyed as instructed. "Then Ananias went to the house and entered it" (v. 17). Ready to be used by the Lord, he went without delay. Humanly speaking, it may have seemed he was putting his head in the lion's mouth. But there are no boundaries to the heart that loves. Obedience is the flip side of the coinage of love.

Ananias' response allowed him to participate in God's answer to Saul's prayers: a vision and a messenger—assurance and confirmation. The Lord goes before His messenger. Saul was so prepared by the vision from God that Ananias found him ready and waiting.

Armed with love, Ananias went in the spirit of Christ. The tenderness of Jesus was felt in Ananias' manner: "Placing his hands on Saul, he said, 'Brother Saul'" (v. 17). It is well to remember, "There is always a confirming clinch given to the faith of a repentant sinner when the clasp of a warm hand receives him into the family of God."[4]

The real proof of our faith is in the touch of our lives. Every day brings opportunity to touch people's lives. What happens? When Jesus touched people, something happened! If we have the spirit of Christ, things will happen, too. That's part of the thrill and privilege of discipling young Christians.

Bishop Francis McConnell received a critical letter. At the peak of denunciation, the letter writer said, "The only thing I can say about you is that you are a skunk." Then the critic signed his letter with these pious words, "Yours in Christ." The whole thing sounds contradictory—for genuine love marks the man "in Christ."

Ananias oozed with the spirit of Jesus: "Brother Saul!" "Brother Saul" rings with human forgiveness, an echo of divine forgiveness. Already Saul felt loved by those whom he had hated. The greatest happiness of life is the conviction that we are loved—loved in spite of ourselves!

In the Jewish Talmud, three rabbis discuss how one can tell when dawn has arrived. One rabbi declares, "It is dawn when you can tell a dog from a wolf."

Another defines dawn as "that moment when you can distinguish blue thread on green cloth."

The third replies, "You know dawn has arrived when you are able to see your brother."

The dawning of love enables one to see his brother!

Armed with love, Ananias represented Jesus. "Brother Saul, the Lord—Jesus, who appeared to you on the road as you were coming here—has sent me" (v. 17). On Jesus' behalf, Ananias confirmed Christ's commission to Saul. Interpreting Saul's amazing experience, he translated the blinding light into the Lord's direction for Saul. People may have many kinds of experiences, but how needful for growing Christians to give direction to the new follower of Jesus. Experience can produce bewilderment—that's where Ananias is needed today! He must help the young convert to translate his new life into terms of mission.

Though Saul became a public figure, preaching and traveling, Ananias was just as indispensable to God as the apostle Paul. The pastor and teacher may be "up front," where people see and hear, but the person who obediently disciples ✓ new Christians has just as important a role. All of us are linked together by God's calling and distribution of spiritual gifts for building His Church.

One must ask, "Am I willing to represent Jesus? Will I prepare myself to be a spiritual parent?"

Haralan Popov, later imprisoned by Bulgarian Communists, told of his conversion in his book, *Tortured for His Faith:*

> A spiritual struggle began within me that lasted many days. The question was: Is there a God? In the Greek Orthodox Church of that time the priests didn't need to have any schooling and only men and women attended the services. You never saw any educated people believing in God. At least, that was the way we atheists like to think. We who had an education looked down on those "simple" men and women who claimed to have "religion" or believed in God. And now I heard educated and cultured people openly testifying that God exists! They told what Christ meant to them and had done for them. This impressed me more than all the sermons, and, to this day, I am a strong believer in the effectiveness of "living testimonies" in bringing men to Christ.
>
> I discussed my conflict with Christo and he said he would introduce me to a man who could help me. Shortly after, Christo invited a man to visit us. His name was Petroff. He read to us from his Bible. He was not an eloquent preacher but every word he uttered proved to me that God existed. He witnessed of how he knew God's personal presence. When he told of what Christ meant to him, his face shone with the love of God. It was obvious to me at that moment that there was a God.
>
> I saw Him in this godly man.
>
> Petroff's testimony convinced me of God's existence and I began earnestly and intensively to seek God. I found I wasn't so much seeking God as God was seeking me. I received a wonderful life-changing experience of

31

salvation in Jesus Christ, and Petroff became my spiritual father.[5]

When testimonies are backed up by godly living, spiritual parenting can and will take place.

Armed with love, Ananias went to bring wholeness. "Jesus . . . has sent me so that you may see again and be filled with the Holy Spirit" (v. 17). Saul's physical sight would be restored and his spiritual blindness would be removed: old, stubborn beliefs; ingrained prejudice; deep-seated religious pride. God would equip Saul with the fullness of the Holy Spirit. It has been noted, "There were no tongues, no sign, no manifestation; there was simply a quiet infilling of the Holy Spirit."[6] Saul was made whole!

Armed with love, Ananias welcomed and initiated Saul into the fellowship of the Church. "Immediately something like scales fell from Saul's eyes, and he could see again. He got up and was baptized" (v. 18).

Under the guidance of his discipler, Saul openly made a profession of his new faith in Christ. The public announcement was sealed by water baptism—symbol of repentance and new life in Christ. By baptism, Saul identified himself with those who follow Jesus. Officially, Saul became a member of the new community of Christians. Ananias welcomed Saul into the family of God!

The story of Ananias is the account of one man who took seriously the Great Commission: "Go and make disciples of all nations, baptizing them in the name of the Father and of the Son and of the Holy Spirit, and teaching them to obey everything I have commanded you" (Matt. 28:19-20). He was willing to obey God and start with one man—a man desperately needing someone to care and to guide in his early days as a Christian.

The Church today needs disciplers. It costs less to train 100 new Christians in godly living than it costs to deal with one average criminal. The believer must arm himself with God's kind of love and be available for His directions. There's a young, struggling Christian somewhere looking for someone to disciple him.

A Chinese proverb says, "Tell me, I'll forget. Show me, I may remember. But involve me and I'll understand!"

CHAPTER 3

Make Use of Your Failure

Acts 9:19-30

As a result of Ananias becoming Saul's spiritual big brother, "Saul spent several days with the disciples in Damascus" (v. 19). The disciples' feelings had to be transformed before they could eat and pray with Saul, whom they feared. The Church expressed forgiving love. Saul responded to their openness and vulnerability.

Jesus' words describe two aspects of Christian development: "Come to me, all you who are weary and burdened, and I will give you rest. Take my yoke upon you and learn from me" (Matt. 11:28-29). First, there's the coming to Jesus. Second, there's the learning from Jesus. Saul had responded to Jesus' invitation to "come." Three days later he was filled with the Holy Spirit and baptized. Equipped for Christian living, the new Saul was zealous to get on with Christian conquest. Unfortunately, he rushed the "learning from Jesus" process. Saul was fired up but needed time for maturity.

In Acts 9:19-30, Luke portrays Saul's zealous effort without knowledge, his attempt to tell it before he really knew it.

With much to learn of Jesus, there are no "6 easy steps" or "10 easy lessons." However, one can learn from failure—Saul's or one's own!

Saul carried his zealous demeanor over from Pharisaism into the gospel. His enthusiasm was admirable; certainly he was never neutral. After all, said F. Lincicome, "God never intended His Church to be a refrigerator in which to preserve perishable piety. He intended it to be an incubator in which to hatch converts." As Peter Marshall added, "A different world cannot be built by indifferent people." But God wants spiritual fruit—not religious nuts!

A young lady, being a baby Christian, asked a distinguished-looking man downtown, "Are you a Christian?"

Politely he responded, "I'm a professor in the theological seminary."

With fire in her eyes, she pressed on, "Brother, you can't let a little thing like that stand in your way!"

The professor admired her zeal—but, of course, zealous workers risk failure. Yet that's not as bad as the failure of doing nothing.

An uneducated man with no church background had recently been introduced to Jesus. Eager and excited about serving God, he begged his pastor to give him something to do for his Lord.

After several pleas, the pastor gave him a stack of church stationery, envelopes, and a roll of postage stamps. He suggested the fellow try writing to people on the inactive list, those disinterested members.

The young Christian diligently began writing letters to encourage the nonattenders to come to church, to get involved, and to start tithing.

One day the pastor received a letter: "Dear Pastor: Thanks for the recent letter from your office. I promise you that I'll be in church next Sunday. You can count on me to be faithful. I'll help in any way I can. Here's my check for last year's unpaid tithe. . . . P.S. Please tell your helper there are not two *t*'s in 'dirty,' and there are no *c*'s in 'skunk.'"

Likewise, Saul's enthusiasm carried him beyond his preparedness.

In His Zeal, Saul Was Hasty

"At once he began to preach in the synagogues that Jesus is the Son of God. All those who heard him were astonished and asked, 'Isn't he the man who raised havoc in Jerusalem among those who call on this name? And hasn't he come here to take them as prisoners to the chief priests?'" (vv. 20-21).

Saul may have begun preaching too soon. God has to build the man before the man can build a sermon. Zeal without knowledge is like haste to a man in the dark!

Though not fearful, Saul was heading for failure. He was attempting to do God's work in his own strength and in his own knowledge. When Jesus had instructed His Church to teach the new disciples to "obey everything I have commanded you" (Matt. 28:19-20), this was more than getting people saved. New Christians need guidance in the disciplines of learning about Jesus and getting to know Him. However, Saul jumped ahead of the Lord by preaching without preparation.

A sporting goods store hired a golf pro to give lessons to new customers. One day two women approached him. He asked one of them, "Would you like to learn to play golf, Madam?"

"Oh, no; not me. My friend wants to learn now," she answered. "Don't you remember? I learned to play yesterday!"

My mother asked a young man who was a new member of the church, "Do you play the piano?"

He replied, "I don't know. I've never tried!"

There's no zeal like the enthusiasm of a new Christian!

He burns with a great desire to be all things for God, to be used for God and the church. However, the church must exercise wisdom and protect him from unnecessary failure. He deserves to be discipled and prepared for Christian living and Christian service.

Saul assumed God wanted him to rescue the Jews. Zealously he decided it was up to him to straighten out the Jews in Damascus. There's nothing wrong in a desire to see people won to Jesus. But God has His own timing. Speed isn't everything; direction counts, too. To see the need does not necessarily constitute a call.

Peter often attempted to put his zeal into action—and not always with good results. In the Garden of Gethsemane, when men came to arrest Jesus, Peter drew his sword and slashed away. His bold stroke only chopped off the ear of the high priest's servant. And that's all the good that well- ✓ intentioned Christians do sometimes, trying to serve God in the energy of the flesh: they go around severing receptive communication with tactless and insensitive strokes. Gratefully, the Lord, in spite of us, can restore receptive ears—and our witnessing *may* have a second chance.

In His Haste, Saul Was Frustrated

Burning with enthusiasm, Saul discovered he's not so hot! At this point, Saul left Damascus to get away to think and pray through his frustration. Luke doesn't mention this interlude in the Book of Acts, but Paul speaks of it in his letter to the Galatian Christians: "But I went immediately into Arabia and later returned to Damascus" (Gal. 1:17).

It seems Saul must have really been frustrated to stay in the desert three years. Apparently he needed solitude and quietness for his searching soul. Too often persons have jumped into an area of ministry, trying to open the deep things of God before they themselves have experienced it. Arnold Airhart noted, "The complete break with the old life, the old associations, the old way of thinking, must have been a traumatic experience. His whole Pharisaic system of religious thought lay shattered at his feet. Time in the desert solitude was needed to think through the implications of Jesus as Messiah, Saviour, and Lord. Especially he pondered the righteousness of God which is God's gift apart from the law, through faith in Jesus Christ."[1]

It was a time of discovery and relearning: "As he began to read through the Old Testament again, he saw Jesus Christ on every page. Everywhere he turned, the Old Testament was speaking of Jesus. In the Prophets, in the Psalms, in Moses and the Law—everywhere it pointed to Jesus. Paul began to discover that the sacrifices and offerings were all pictures of Jesus. The very configuration of the Tabernacle was a picture of the life of Jesus. Jesus was everywhere throughout the Old Testament."[2]

The more Saul studied, the more he got enthused—and got frustrated with preparation time: "There's a nation to be saved—and here I sit in the desert. I've got to get going!" And he may have returned too soon. By failing to prepare, one may be preparing to fail.

Saul became more frustrated by the Jews' failure to accept what was so clear to him. "Yet Saul grew more and more powerful and baffled the Jews living in Damascus by proving that Jesus is the Christ" (v. 22). He was sure he had the answers to wipe out all opposition to Jesus as Messiah. So he went forth to prove it!

The Greek word for "proving" comes from an older word meaning "to knit together." Jesus' life and ministry were knitted together with the Old Testament Scriptures. Saul "joined them together" by putting the Old Testament Scriptures alongside their fulfillment in Jesus. Saul could see so clearly—and he told them so. He concluded that they should see it as well as he. Wrong! Saul was running ahead of the Holy Spirit who alone is the Revealer of God's truth.

Saul became frustrated by lack of success. One writer commented, "[Saul] wins all the battles, but loses the war. He wins all the arguments, but he never wins a soul. In spite of his tremendous dedication, in spite of the skillful and knowledgeable arguments he employs, in spite of the untiring, sincere effort of this dedicated, zealous young man, the Jews remain locked in stubborn and obstinate unbelief."[3]

Yes, Saul provoked responses from people—but no conversions. Some "were astonished" (v. 20). It means literally, "They stood outside of themselves in amazement." It was like standing to one side and saying, "I can't believe what I'm hearing!" Perhaps they applauded. The reward for human effort is applause. The reward for spiritual effort is changed lives!

Sam Jones had surgery on his liver. After awakening, his surgeon asked, "How does your side feel?"

"Oh, my side's all right," Jones croaked. "But I have a terrible pain in my throat. What's wrong with me?"

"Well," sighed the doctor, "I operate in a big amphitheater filled with students and interns. It's tense with all those eyes watching every cut and stitch! Yours was a most unusual case. Some doctors never see it in a lifetime. During the long procedure my hand was steady. I had perfect results.

"When it was over and I stepped back from the table, the crowd burst into applause. The medical students stood on their feet and cheered. In fact, the acclaim was so loud and long, that—well, Jones—I took out your tonsils for an encore!"

The remainder of Saul's audience was "baffled" (v. 22) or confounded. The Greek word for "baffled" means "to pour together, to commingle." They were mixed up! The more Saul argued, the more confused they became!

Why? Saul was fighting in the power of the flesh! He was trying "real hard" to do God's work for Him. It was "a good campaign, marred only by failure!"

39

Like Saul in Damascus, we are headed for failure attempting to do God's work when we are out of the stream of His Spirit! While God is patient, we frustrate ourselves and others!

In His Frustration, Saul Was Humiliated

Saul was humiliated because his listeners would rather get rid of him than follow his message: "After many days had gone by, the Jews conspired to kill him" (v. 23). Since Saul had deserted their ideals, they met secretly and passed a resolution to eliminate him. According to Paul's testimony later, the Jews involved the governor in the plot: "In Damascus the governor under King Aretas had the city of the Damascenes guarded in order to arrest me" (2 Cor. 11:32).

Saul's humiliation mounted when he had to leave in secrecy. He had come so dramatically—what an ignominious exit! Zealous, rushing in to the rescue, frustrated by lack of success, humiliated with disgrace, Saul is a failure! "But I was lowered in a basket from a window in the wall and slipped through his hands" (2 Cor. 11:33). Saul had come to show how much he could do for Jesus—and he slunk away into darkness utterly defeated.

Saul is about to hit bottom. He's almost at the end of his rope. And God still loves him and accepts him—even with his imperfect performance. Saul is no quitter. Stubbornly he is going to try one more time to perform successfully in his own strength.

Leaving Damascus behind in the night, Saul goes back the 200 miles to Jerusalem. It has been at least three years since he left there. But Jerusalem is where he was trained and began his career. People know him around Jerusalem—and he can impress them for Jesus!

Unexpectedly, Saul is again humiliated. The disciples of Jesus reject him! His past life had caught up with him: "When he came to Jerusalem, he tried to join the disciples, but they

40

were all afraid of him, not believing that he really was a disciple" (v. 26). His new fellow believers viewed him as a persecutor; his old friends saw him as a traitor. Saul's greatest obstacle became his own past. He would have to face it. One writer noted, "All of us make mistakes, do foolish things, and sin. As we repent, God graciously forgives us and forgets our past. But men are not always ready to forget, and it may take a Christian a long time to live down wasted years or even a moment of folly or a few careless words."[4] But not in God's eyes!

Even so, Saul "tried to join the disciples." The Greek verb for "join" always describes close, intimate fellowship. It portrays the deep bond between husband and wife, between real brothers, and between cherished friends. Saul was seeking fellowship with the disciples. It is always easier to join outwardly than to enter that deep, satisfying fellowship. However, the disciples were fearful. They remained at arm's length. What a disillusioning experience that must have been!

At this point the story takes a turn for the better: "But Barnabas took him and brought him to the apostles. He told them how Saul on his journey had seen the Lord and that the Lord had spoken to him, and how in Damascus he had preached fearlessly in the name of Jesus" (v. 27).

Barnabas took a risk—love always takes risks. Barnabas always seems to trust people. I think that's the result of believing greatly in God! Forgiveness and confidence flow from Barnabas to Saul.

Believing Saul to be a diamond in the rough, Barnabas took Saul by the hand and led him into the fellowship of believers. Risking his life and reputation, he befriended Saul. And every new Christian needs a Barnabas, a "Son of Encouragement." Goethe said, "Encouragement after censure is as the sun after a shower." I need someone to believe in me

41

even when the crowd is in doubt. We all need someone to put courage into us.

Words spoken at Gandhi's funeral also describe Barnabas: "He was great, yes. But he was more than great; he was good. He troubled the world by his goodness."

Then and now, the Church must be redemptive: "So Saul stayed with them" (v. 28). We, too, must err on the side of forgiving love! We must gamble on people. Occasionally we will be disappointed, but the story of Christianity is the story of God who takes chances on people with a bad record. God does not hold our past sins and failures against us. And we, too, should never condemn a person because he failed!

For 15 days in Jerusalem, Saul humiliated himself even more. He considered himself as Stephen's replacement and went around visiting the same synagogues where Stephen had spoken: "He talked and debated with the Grecian Jews, but they tried to kill him" (v. 29). Saul bounded from one dispute to another, arguing and debating.

The whole Jerusalem scene for Saul is a repetition of his failure in Damascus—trying to do God's work in his own wisdom. At least Saul was getting experience—that wonderful ability to recognize a mistake when we make it again!

> To err is human
> But not sublime.
> Just don't make boo-boos
> The second time!

Saul hit bottom at last. He failed enough to know he would have to trust God completely.

In His Humiliation, Saul Listened to God

Paul tells about it later in the Book of Acts: "When I returned to Jerusalem and was praying at the temple, I fell into a trance and saw the Lord speaking. 'Quick!' he said to me. 'Leave Jerusalem immediately, because they will not accept your testimony about me'" (22:17-18).

Saul attempts to argue with the Lord: "'Lord,' I replied, 'these men know that I went from one synagogue to another to imprison and beat those who believe in you. And when the blood of your martyr Stephen was shed, I stood there giving my approval and guarding the clothes of those who were killing him.'

"Then the Lord said to me, 'Go; I will send you far away to the Gentiles'" (22:19-21). God had a different idea than Saul about his ministry—a different time and a different place and a different people! Saul would have to learn to depend upon the Lord totally.

At about the same time: "When the brothers learned of this [the attempt to kill Saul], they took him down to Caesarea and sent him off to Tarsus" (v. 30). Fellow Christians stood by Saul and protected him—even from himself. God was at work through Christian friends. They hurried him off to Caesarea, Israel's major seaport, and sent him 300 miles north to Tarsus, his hometown.

God was working behind the scenes and Saul could testify later, "And we know that in all things God works for the good of those who love him" (Rom. 8:28). God is still at work behind the scenes of each person's life. If at first one does not succeed, he should try looking in God's Handbook for instructions. The Lord desires His child to learn to depend on Him. That's why sometimes He doesn't stop us from hitting bottom. God meets us at our point of failure. Never fear failure; God is there!

God guided Saul back through four stages in his life. He took him away from his Arabian loneliness; back through Damascus, the place of his conversion; back through Jerusalem, the place of his training and career; and then back to Tarsus, his native land.

Probably Saul went home defeated, feeling like Enrico

43

Caruso at his audition for the La Scala Opera. At 21 years of age, Caruso was so frightened, his voice trembled. He sang dismally. Weeping on his teacher's shoulder, he sobbed, "I have failed, Maestro. Never will I sing again!"

But failure is not final. Failure is not fatal. And he did sing again and again—until he had sung his way into the hearts of millions around the world.

We come to the greatest gap in Saul's career since we first met him at Stephen's death. Saul is lost from view for eight long years. All one can say is that the Lord knew best. God never lost Saul's address! Apparently it was a time of preparation so desperately needed for Saul's illustrious future. Dr. Lloyd Ogilvie adds, "Times of preparation on the Way are often lonely and painful. But the Lord knew what He was doing. . . . Often I have been impatient, longing to get on with changing the world, but the Lord had to change me first. When I look back to those times out of the mainstream of what I thought the Lord was doing, I can see that I was being prepared for the fast-moving currents which later carried me out to the high seas of adventure and effectiveness. The Lord will not use us until He has made us ready. Then we thank Him for knowing what He was doing."[5]

In the battlefields of human failure, one name comes ringing and singing over the stilled wrecks of disappointment: "Jesus! Jesus! Jesus!" Jesus never abandoned Saul when he failed. And He is still in control. The Chinese word for "Jesus" means "The One who saves again and again." Our Lord rescues again and again even though we fail. Like Saul we have had our times of failure—but Jesus has never failed to lift us and love us and give new hope.

English chemist Sir Humphrey Davy said, "The most important of my discoveries have been suggested to me by my failures." Let God use our failures to bring fresh discoveries of His grace and power!

Gloria Gaither captured the truth in song:

Something beautiful, something good;
All my confusion He understood.
All I had to offer Him was brokenness and strife,
But He made something beautiful of my life.*

CHAPTER 4

"... and All Is Well!"

Acts 9:31-43

On Easter Sunday of 1941, the famous City Temple in London was crowded with worshipers. Little did they know that would be their last Sunday of worship in their famous building. On the following Thursday the building was gutted by German bombs. The next Sunday morning the congregation met in a rented hall. In spite of losses and damage, the church sang their morning hymn:

> *Lead us, Heavenly Father, lead us*
> *O'er the world's tempestuous sea.*
> *Guard us, guide us, keep us, feed us,*
> *For we have no help but Thee;*
> *Yet possessing every blessing,*
> *Our God our Helper be.*

A building belonging to the church can be destroyed—but the Church cannot. It is God's own possession.

After sketching the explosion, persecution, and expansion of the Church, Luke pauses at Acts 9:31 to survey the battle and call out, "... and all is well!" With Saul the persecutor converted to the Way of Jesus and sent back home to Tarsus, Luke gives a progress report on "the state of the church": "Then the church throughout Judea, Galilee and Sa-

maria enjoyed a time of peace. It was strengthened; and encouraged by the Holy Spirit, it grew in numbers, living in the fear of the Lord" (v. 31).

Thus closes the first period of the Christian Church—from its birth at the Pentecost festival following Jesus' ascension to the resurrection of Dorcas—a probable period of about eight years. Persecution seemed to fade; the Church experienced a temporary time of peace and rest.

Notice that Luke writes about the Church and not "the churches." Local gatherings of believers are expressions of the Church. A local church should visibly demonstrate Christ's Church to that community. Geographical and ecclesiastical designations simply identify various parts of the Body of Christ. If there is but one God, one Christ, one Cross, one Holy Spirit, there is but one Church!

Surviving persecution and crossing political borders, the Church remained alive and well. Let's examine Luke's progress report on the Church.

The Church Was Being Constructed on Firm Foundations

"It was strengthened" (v. 31). One translator said the Church was "being constantly built up" (Wuest). Some use the word "edified," which describes the orderly and progressive growth of a building structure being raised up from the right foundations. The Bible portrays the Church as "God's household, built on the foundation of the apostles and prophets, with Christ Jesus himself as the chief cornerstone. In him the whole building is joined together and rises to become a holy temple in the Lord. And in him you too are being built together to become a dwelling in which God lives by his Spirit" (Eph. 2:19-22). Christians moved the Temple out of center and became God's temple wherever they went.

The local church must be built on firm foundations. In condensed form our foundation blocks appear in the Apostles' Creed—taken from God's Word—indestructible foundations. We must remain dogmatic about our foundations, for "when the foundations are being destroyed, what can the righteous do?" (Ps. 11:3).

When I go to the pharmacist to have a prescription filled, I want him to be dogmatic about the proportions of ingredients. When I need a doctor, I want him to be dogmatic about how to get me well. When I fly in an airliner, I want the most dogmatic pilot that jet airplane ever had. I want him to be dogmatic about doing what the control tower man commands him. I want him to go by his instruments—not his emotions. I want him to fly by true and tested navigation—not his momentary whims. And I want to hear a preacher who preaches dogmatic sermons about a dogmatic Bible! The dogma or doctrines of the Bible are infallible about how I can get to know Jesus and go to heaven with Him!

Some people attempt to build on their own opinions or emotions. Their brand of religion reminds me of the fellow who put one chair on top of another. Standing insecurely on this shaky base, he was attempting to drive a nail into the wall, but could only give it ineffectual taps.

His wife said, "Strike a brave blow, husband!"

He replied, "I cannot strike a brave blow on such a shaky foundation!"

The Church of Acts 9 was being built up. The Greek verb for "being built up," *oikodomeo*, came from two words, *oikos* (house), and *demo* (to build). It means literally, "to build a house." On top of true foundations, His Church was being built up one course of block at a time—like a stonemason or bricklayer progressively building higher as the structure rises a step at a time. Each Christian fits into the whole, being benefited by those before him.

The grammar suggests the Church *"being* built up." It carries the idea of incompleteness. Luke had no idea of the church as a completed project. It was and is still being built.

That thought carries the idea of progress, looking forward to a completion date which only God knows. And today, the Church is still being built. If only we would remember that, we would quit criticizing His Church. It is not completed; it is being built. Half the things we quarrel about today among churches is scaffolding, not the building!

Many people think the Church is a museum in which to display finished saints. The Church is really a workshop where Christian character is being produced. None of us needs to feel we must be a completed project before joining the church. A bumper sticker puts it well: "Please be patient with me; God is not finished with me yet."

The Church Was Being Committed to Obedience to God

The church was "living in the fear of the Lord" (v. 31). The Bible has repeatedly emphasized in one way or another: "The fear of the Lord is the beginning of knowledge" (Prov. 1:7). It means the believer must have a reverential awe of God. God is not just a pal, an object of sentimental affections. He is more than a celestial nice neighbor. We must respect and reverence Him. God desires more than a tip of our hat or a nod of our recognition of Him. God is all-powerful, a holy God, a God of justice deeply displeased with our intentional disobedience.

The biblical concept of "the fear of the Lord" carries the idea that the Church "dreaded to do anything that might displease and offend the Lord. In their daily life and walk the members had Jesus present with them. . . . this strong motive is largely absent today; church members too often persuade themselves that the Lord does not mind their worldliness and love of praise from men."[1]

Followers of Jesus are motivated to obey the Lord. Out of love and respect they wish to do whatever pleases Him. It is not obedience out of fear, but obedience out of respect and reverence which seeks to give immediate response to His commands. The Early Church was sensitive to the directions of the Lord.

"Living in the fear of the Lord" can also mean *"walking* in the fear of the Lord." The Church was "going on its way." The Greek word for "living" or "walking" suggests a sense of direction in its progress. Another Greek word found in the New Testament for "walking" carries the idea of aimlessly walking around. But not this word (v. 31). Jesus used this one in the Great Commission: "Therefore *go* and make disciples of all nations" (Matt. 28:19). We must be busy going about our Father's business. Walking with Him, we go in His direction. Let's keep in step with Jesus!

The Church Was Being Coached by the Holy Spirit

Luke said the Church was "encouraged by the Holy Spirit" (v. 31). The Church needs not only that reverential awe of the Lord but also the Holy Spirit's help, enabling us to do God's work.

Only here in the Book of Acts does Luke use the word *paraclesis* to describe the work and ministry of the Holy Spirit. In John's Gospel, Jesus spoke much about the "Comforter" (KJV) promised to believers. It is the same basic word meaning "one who consoles, one offering encouragement, one called to our side, one giving enthusiastic help." The various shades of meaning of *paraclete* seem to describe a coach who can infuse excitement and courage and zeal into the sagging spirits of his men. The Holy Spirit is called to our side to help us in every way. He is our Advisor, our Helper, our Encourager.

No doubt the Early Church needed encouragement and the lifting up of sagging spirits through the tragic days of persecution. The Holy Spirit was faithful to "enthuse" His people. The New Testament Church was the community of the Spirit.

50

Dr. E. P. Ellyson told of a little boy and his dog who got separated at a ballpark one afternoon. The frightened little dog searched for his master. He got through a hole in the fence and ended up on the baseball diamond just before the game started. The stands were filled with spectators milling around—a sea of confusion to the pup. Some began whistling and yelling at the unhappy hound. It all added to his confusion. Frightened and muddled by the pandemonium, the dog didn't know which way to go.

Few people noticed the boy who crawled through the same hole in the fence and was coming up behind the dog. Amid all the noise and distractions, the boy put his hand on his little dog's head and whispered, "Come on, Sport. Let's go home!"

The loving touch and the familiar voice of his master changed the downcast dog into a bundle of enthusiasm. While people watched, the boy and his dog walked away, ignoring the crowd, and went home together in joy!

That's a parable of the Holy Spirit's work in the heart of His people. Amid all the catcalls and competing voices—and even the solemn silences of rejection—the Spirit gives His touch of reassurance. He whispers encouragement to our hearts and leads us on in His sweet fellowship. The Spirit of God gives us heart. "When I need Him, He is there!"

The Church Was Being Contagious as an Epidemic

Luke noted that the Church "grew in numbers" (v. 31). J. B. Phillips translated: "It became established and as it went forward in reverence for the Lord and in the strengthening presence of the Holy Spirit, continued to grow in numbers." The KJV uses the mathematical language "were multiplied." New life in Christ swept through the country like an epidemic!

Persevering in the face of incredible odds, the Early Church did not *support* missionaries; the people *were* missionaries! The Early Church was a missionary movement. When the Church is strengthened with the encouraging voice of the Holy Spirit, it will multiply. In addition to spiritual growth, the Church was being built numerically. The increased numbers of people turning to Jesus was evidence of the Spirit's power at work through witnessing men and women.

In mathematics, multiplication is a more dynamic concept than addition. Multiplication starts slower than addition—but given just a little time, there's no comparison. One plus one equals two—that's addition. One times one equals one—that's multiplication. But just wait! Multiplying soon outdistances adding. The process of discipling men and multiplying starts slower at first than just adding converts. But just wait!

A wealthy man gave his little son a choice for a birthday present. He could have a $100 bill or a penny doubled each day for one month. The lad chose the crisp, new $100 bill. Had he chosen the penny doubled each day for 30 days, he could have received $10,737,417. (My pocket calculator cancelled out on the 34th day. It couldn't compute that much money.)

Too often the church has settled for its pastor to add occasional converts—but the Bible talks about the church multiplying!

A Tanzanian, converted while visiting Kenya, returned home and began telling his friends about Christ. Six years later, 8,400 converts and 30 churches populated his area. Several men were training to be pastors.

Some folk argue, "We shouldn't be concerned with numbers." But in church, each number is a person—and that number is very important to me if it is my wife or daughter! A healthy child grows and so must a healthy church. The church must be "being built up" and, as a result, it will be "being multiplied." If the church is to be missionary, it must be spiritual. If the church is to be spiritual, it must be missionary.

William S. Knudsen said, "A big corporation is more or less blamed for being big. It is big only because it gives service. If it doesn't give service, it gets small faster than it grew." These words could be well said of the church.

Christians must keep that person-to-person contact of love and witness for Jesus Christ.

The Church Was Being Crowned with Evidences of God's Power

In verses 32-35, Luke gives an example of some of the exciting things happening through the Church. People were getting help. God was at work.

Peter, on tour through the country, came to Christians at Lydda. There Peter met a man paralyzed for eight years. Sensing God's power, Peter said, "Jesus Christ heals you. Get up and arrange your things" (v. 34, author's paraphrase). The man got right up—healed and made whole! As a result, many others "turned to the Lord" (v. 35).

Why Aeneas was made whole but others not—only God knows the redemptive purposes behind it. However, human need was met and others were brought into the kingdom of God as a result.

Peter's words to Aeneas are fitting as the church meets in worship today. The force of the Greek grammar is: "This instant Jesus Christ is healing you!" It is a present touch of wholeness. And in our midst as we pray together, sing together, and open ourselves to God's Word together, Jesus brings His touch of healing and wholeness to someone.

Out of an unidentified magazine I cut these words: "The church attracts because of its healing ministry. The writer said to a doctor, 'I observe that you and most other doctors never do any advertising. You have only a small sign at the entrance to your office, yet you have all the patients you can care for.'

"He explained that sometimes a physician finds it a little slow when he starts. But he said, 'When a doctor does something to relieve a person, giving aid to his health, that person does not forget. When he or his friends need medical assistance, he remembers; and that is our best advertising.' People will go a long way to their favorite doctor or hospital."

If God's healing touch is allowed to flow through His Church, people will get help and others shall come to know Jesus!

In verses 36-42, Peter goes to the neighboring town of Joppa, now a suburb of modern Tel Aviv. Dorcas, known also by her Hebrew name, Tabitha, had gotten sick and died. She was a Christian "who was always doing good" (v. 36). Her full heart had inspired her deft fingers. She had helped by sewing garments for the poor. Her example has inspired ladies around the world to form sewing circles to assist needy people and missions. Luccock said Dorcas was "founder of an International Ladies Garment Workers' Union, one of the greatest labor unions of all times, with branches in all lands." She had habitually performed mercy deeds, acts of kindness.

Tragically it ended when she died suddenly. When Peter arrived at her home, the widows were brokenhearted at losing such a friend. They showed Peter the very dresses they were wearing—handiwork of Dorcas. How deeply they grieved! Again, sensing God's direction, Peter sent all the mourners out of the room. He needed an atmosphere of faith. He had a deep assurance from the Lord as he prayed. A miracle took place! Dorcas was raised from the dead!

Of course, that miracle was only temporary. Dorcas would someday die again. But the miracle was a symbol and sign that the risen Christ had power of life and death, that He would do unusual things through His Church. Jesus has conquered death! "This became known all over Joppa, and many people believed in the Lord" (v. 42). Again, God did the unique, the unusual, for His own redemptive purposes.

God still transforms the lives of people in the climate of a healthy, Spirit-filled church. Many dead in their trespasses and sins shall experience new life in Christ. It will have the ring of eternity! "Whenever the risen Christ is present, there is new power to overcome the handicaps of human existence. Miracles do happen. They happened then and they happen now."[2] These experiences sound like what Jesus did when He walked among men. And He himself promised that His disciples would do even greater things!

The Church survived its first wave of persecution. Luke leans from the tower of his perspective, shouting, ". . . and all is well!" The Church must continue serving and teaching in the name of the Lord Jesus Christ. In the Book of Acts, the Church put on its boots and working clothes. God gave His men legs in order to walk the ways of human need. He gave them hands to lift and bless. The Church was "the fellowship of people who cared; a new cult of concern."

What is the main business of the Church? To make Christ real to every generation—to present the God we see unmistakably in Jesus to a staggering, weary, and undeserving humanity.

CHAPTER 5

"At Your Service, Lord!"

Acts 10:1-23

A pastor met a little boy and asked, "Who made you?"

The lad replied, "To tell the truth, sir, I ain't done yet!" He was still growing. The longer he would live, the more opportunity life would give for growth.

At the end of Acts 9, Peter isn't done yet—Peter is still being made over by God's grace. He is in a strange place for a Jew—staying in Joppa with "a tanner named Simon" (Acts 9:43).

Peter is a follower of Jesus, filled with the Holy Spirit, but eight years after Pentecost still a victim of prejudice against Gentiles. All changes do not happen suddenly and automatically when a person is filled with the Spirit. For example, prejudice experiences a slow, lingering death. It is deeply embedded into one's mind during formative years. Prejudices keep people separate from those they fear or do not know.

Peter lived in a world of prejudice. Deep emotional barriers existed between Jew and Gentile, between men and women, between Roman and non-Roman (the conquerors and the conquered), between Greek and non-Greek (the cultured and those considered barbarians), between free man and slave, between the ignorant man and the wise man. Everywhere in the ancient world barriers labeled people "common" or "unclean."

For a Jew, entering a tanner's home marked defilement. Since a tanner handled dead skins and carcasses, his trade was considered "unclean." His house must be located no less than 75 yards outside the city limits. In fact, a girl engaged to a tanner without knowledge of his business, upon discovery could obtain an annulment.

Residing in a tanner's house, Peter gives evidence that prejudices were being broken down gradually. In Joppa a good Christian man traditionally considered an outcast was kind enough to entertain Peter. That was unsettling to Peter's preconceived ideas. His Jewish exclusiveness was melting away.

Amazingly, God was preparing Peter for the next important step of the Church of Jesus Christ. The following episode (Acts 10:23-48) finds Peter going to the home of a Gentile Roman officer and welcoming him into God's family. That had never been done before!

In writing the Book of Acts, Luke treats this coming event as one of the great crises in Early Church history. Luke described Cornelius' vision four times and Peter's vision twice. Not only is Acts 10 devoted to this major development, but Acts 11:5-18 contains a summary of the whole encounter, and Acts 15 settles the issue. It is difficult to overestimate the importance of this event. The break between Judaism and Christianity is signaled. Judaism was the religion of a nation. Christianity is a religion for "whosoever will." The break had to come!

The meeting of Peter and Cornelius marks a new era. For the first time, a Gentile is publicly and officially welcomed into the Christian family without being required to conform to Jewish law. It has the echo of prophecy from Peter's sermon at Pentecost: "I will pour out my Spirit on all people" (Acts 2:17).

While Peter stayed in Joppa, God was dealing with a Gentile Roman centurion named Cornelius more than 30 miles north in Caesarea. Located on the shores of the Mediterranean Sea, Caesarea was the official capital of the Roman governor over the province of Judea. Under the governors Pilate, Felix, and Festus, Caesarea was the headquarters for the Roman occupation army.

The Roman army was organized by legions (6,000 men), cohorts (600 men—10 cohorts to a legion), and centuries (100 men—6 centuries to a cohort). A centurion was a noncommissioned officer over 100 men. Centurions were called "the backbone of the Roman army." New Testament writers looked upon them with favor and respect.

Cornelius, centurion of the Italian regiment, became a man who disdained pagan deities prevalent in his culture. Luke says, "He and all his family were devout and God-fearing; he gave generously to those in need and prayed to God regularly" (v. 2). One day an angel appeared and explained, "Your prayers and gifts to the poor have come up as a remembrance before God. Now send men to Joppa to bring back a man named Simon who is called Peter. He is staying with Simon the tanner, whose house is by the sea" (vv. 4-6). The angel gave Cornelius directions and, by mentioning that Peter was staying with a tanner, gave a clue that Peter wasn't all tied up with usual Jewish rigidity.

God was setting the stage for a remarkably new era in the Church. He wasn't through making Peter yet. The Lord was preparing him for an important new lesson. God was going to use Peter in ways he did not suspect. God was working in His man and through His man!

The Master isn't done with us yet. He still desires to prepare each of us for a more effective ministry and wider influence than we can see at the present moment. God is at work, making some things happen, preventing some things from happening, and allowing some things to take place.

How can we be more effective for God? By learning to be sensitive to His guidance and by responding to His leadership. God will not guide us where His grace cannot keep us. We can learn from Peter's experience.

We Must Be Receptive to God's Lessons

God gave Peter these important lessons during his prayer time. "About noon the following day . . . Peter went up on the roof to pray" (v. 9). The flat roofs of Oriental houses were often used as places of meditation and prayer, quiet places away from the noise of crowded houses. God met Peter at his place of prayer.

The Lord unfolds His lessons to those who pray. Prayer is our communication with God by which we report our victories and failures, as well as receive our marching orders. Prayer must not become "using God" but rather should involve reporting for duty! To learn the lessons God is trying to teach us, we will need moments for our appointed times and places to meet with the Lord.

The great clock of St. Paul's Cathedral cannot be heard more than a block or two above the roar of London's traffic as the hour is struck. But, in the silence of night, the clock can be heard striking over a great area. And we need times of silence, listening times, to hear the Voice so often disregarded in the busy walks of life.

Not everyone appreciates the silences. In the monastery where Leonardo da Vinci was painting his *Last Supper* masterpiece, monks grew impatient because he stood in silence by the hour staring at his painting without using his brush. They expected him to work feverishly to complete his work in the shortest possible time. Seeing him stand in silence for so long seemed unproductive to them. At their complaint, da

Vinci replied, "It is when I pause the longest that I make the most telling strokes with my brush."

To learn God's lessons well, we must take time to meet with the Lord in our silent times and places.

God gave Peter a clear picture of God's truth. Thomas A. Carruth commented, "Often the most important thing that happens in prayer takes place when you are not talking at all. The insight, the sense of guidance may come during a time of quiet listening. What God has to say to us is always more important than anything we have to say to Him."[1]

"[Peter] became hungry and wanted something to eat, and while the meal was being prepared, he fell into a trance" (v. 10). During this wide-awake vision, God gave Peter an object lesson: "He saw heaven opened and something like a large sheet being let down to earth by its four corners" (v. 11). The "sheet" described is a nautical term for a "sail." Perhaps Peter had been watching the large sails of fishing fleets from his seaside rooftop, and it became suggestive to his vision.

"It contained all kinds of four-footed animals, as well as reptiles of the earth and birds of the air. Then a voice told him, 'Get up, Peter. Kill and eat'" (vv. 12-13). Jewish law had declared ceremonially "clean" those animals which chew their cud and have cloven hoofs. In Peter's vision, animals considered "unclean" were mixed in—not permissible for a Jew to eat. And, being mixed together, all were then considered "unclean."

The Lord gave Peter this visual object lesson to illustrate that the animals, symbolic of the Church, had originated in heaven. After the vision, "immediately the sheet was taken back to heaven" (v. 16). The destiny of the Church is also heaven. God's Church is broader than Jewish legal limits, beyond traditions and cultures and confines of any nation or race or institution. Those men and women reclaimed by God's grace cannot be discounted or excluded!

God had to change Peter's thinking before He could

change Peter's behavior. Previous to his vision, Peter would never have traveled with three Gentiles to visit another Gentile's house. God was still at work remaking Peter. The Lord's instructions were: "Get up, Peter. Kill and eat" (v. 13).

With all his acquired background and prejudice, Peter argued, "Surely not, Lord! . . . I have never eaten anything impure or unclean" (v. 14). In the King James Version, Peter's words are: "Not so, Lord." Ray Stedman pointed out: "Obviously you cannot be consistent and say, 'Not so, Lord.' If you say 'Lord' then you must not say, 'Not so.' And if you say 'Not so' then He is not Lord!"[2]

Sometimes there is inner conflict between God's guidance and one's cultural backgrounds. But Christianity will burst the wineskins of offending culture and prejudice! If we take the Lordship of Jesus seriously, there will be profound conflicts with our cultural value systems. God changes our hearts in an instant of conversion. But the Lord works at changing our thinking in order to change our behavior. Many of our thought patterns and responses have to be brought under subjection to the Holy Spirit. A perfect heart before the Lord is not equated with perfect judgment or insight. God helps us change the thought life so deeply embedded in our learned responses.

"The voice spoke to [Peter] a second time, 'Do not call anything impure that God has made clean'" (v. 15). God was teaching Peter that His love and mercy extend beyond all barriers. The voice spoke with rebuke to quit calling "no good" what God has redeemed. We must not treat with disrespect or disregard anyone for whom Christ died!

And sometimes we treat ourselves as unclean or worthless. Every pastor has heard good people say, "'I just can't forgive myself. The things I've done are so bad that even though I know God has forgiven me, I can't accept myself.' It often helps if we can see that by this attitude we are calling

God a liar. We are calling unclean what God has called clean."[3]

At a distinguished civic dinner, an elderly man was disconcerted to find himself seated next to a quiet Chinese fellow. Wanting to be courteous, however, he leaned toward the visitor and asked, "Likee soupee?"

The Chinese looked at him, nodded, but said nothing. Later, during the dinner, the Chinese was called upon to speak. He rose, bowed, and made a 15-minute speech in impeccable English about the sociological significance of the European Common Market. Amid polite applause he sat down, turned to his embarrassed Anglo neighbor, and asked quietly, "Likee speechee?"

Let us never be condescending to anyone in the great human family. It is such an important lesson to Peter and to us that the whole drama was repeated three times, a threefold witness fulfilling the Mosaic Law: "A matter must be established by the testimony of two or three witnesses" (Deut. 19:15). The threefold reminder may have jogged Peter's memory of Jesus' threefold command to him: "Feed my sheep" (John 21). The repeated vision illustrated God's loving patience with the infirmities of human weakness and slowness to learn.

We Must Rest in God's Timings

Peter didn't have to wait long. God's timing was perfect: "While Peter was wondering about the meaning of the vision, the men sent by Cornelius found out where Simon's house was and stopped at the gate. They called out, asking if Simon who was known as Peter was staying there" (vv. 17-18).

God is at work behind the scenes. The Lord was making all the arrangements in order to accomplish His purposes. God gave the vision and instructions to Cornelius in Caesarea at precisely the right time for the men to travel more than 30 miles, look up the address of Simon the tanner, and locate Simon Peter—as He had instructed. And they arrived at precisely the right moment!

People speak of "chance" and "coincidence," but I believe in God's timings. The Psalmist expresses that confidence: "O Lord, you have examined my heart and know everything about me. You know when I sit or stand. . . . You chart the path ahead of me, and tell me where to stop and rest. Every moment, you know where I am. . . . You both precede and follow me, and place your hand of blessing on my head. This is too glorious, too wonderful to believe! I can *never* be lost to your Spirit!" (Ps. 139:1-3, 5-7, TLB).

God has His times and places and people and purposes. The Lord brings together those He has been preparing separately; He does this by the leadings of the Holy Spirit. The man in Caesarea is the product of God's light given to Gentiles apart from Judaism. The man in Joppa is the product of Judaism and his living encounter with Jesus. Peter had the background of institutional religion but needed to be set free from its confinement. Cornelius had the background of Gentile freedom but needed discipline and direction. God was beautifully preparing to bring them together for the benefit of both!

The Bible says, "The steps of a good man are ordered by the Lord" (Ps. 37:23, KJV). The Spirit guides those who listen. When we are near enough to God to hear His voice, the Lord's directions are always clear enough to follow!

The eight-year-old son of a New York pastor made an appointment to see his father. It embarrassed his father to think his son had to make an appointment to see him—that's being too busy!

At the appointed hour, the boy arrived, marched into his father's office, and sat down in the big chair. After a pause, he said, "Dad, tell me: Just what do you know about God?"

It was a testing moment. Finally the father answered, "Not much, son; but enough!"

That answer is hard to improve on. If we're talking about the infinite Creator of the universe, "not much." But through Jesus Christ we know enough to rest in God's care and His perfect timing.

William Cowper ordered a carriage to take him to the Thames River; he was so despondent he intended to commit suicide by leaping from the bridge. However, the London fog was so dense the driver got lost. Finally, after an hour of tramping through the cold, swirling fog, Cowper demanded to be let out. As the lines emerged out of the thick night fog, he discovered that he was standing right at his front door! Moved by the caring providence of God, he went in and wrote these words:

> God moves in a mysterious way
>   His wonders to perform;
> He plants His footsteps in the sea,
>   And rides upon the storm.
>
> Ye fearful saints, fresh courage take.
>   The clouds ye so much dread
> Are big with mercy, and shall break
>   In blessings on your head.
>
> Judge not the Lord by feeble sense,
>   But trust Him for His grace;
> Behind a frowning providence
>   He hides a smiling face.

God can be trusted with the timetable of our lives!

We Must Respond to God's Opportunities

God provides opportunities to minister and serve. "While Peter was still thinking about the vision, the Spirit said to him, 'Simon, three men are looking for you. So get up and go downstairs. Do not hesitate to go with them, for I have sent them'" (vv. 19-20).

In Oriental custom, the three men stood outside and called for Simon called Peter. God provided Peter an immediate opportunity to put this amazing object lesson into action!

Any learning program or lesson must find application in the arena of real life. Biblical concepts are given to make a difference in how we live. The Bible is not an ivory-tower tourist guide, but a manufacturer's handbook on how to operate in real life. The Lord provided homework for Peter in Lesson No. 1 immediately. When opportunity knocks at some folks' door, they are in the backyard looking for a lucky four-leaf clover!

God helps His people to recognize opportunities when they come. He sensitizes each disciple to opportunities for service. Many fail to recognize opportunity because it often comes disguised as hard work!

A cartoon shows a pastor sitting on his associate pastor's desk. The poor associate is stretched out wearily. The pastor says, "As my associate, the first thing to learn is that vexations and frustrations are always called 'challenges' and 'opportunities'!"

God interprets His lessons through opportunities to serve: "Peter went down and said to the men, 'I'm the one you're looking for. Why have you come?'

"The men replied, 'We have come from Cornelius the centurion. . . . A holy angel told him to have you come to his house so that he could hear what you have to say'" (vv. 21-22).

The Lord put flesh on the lesson outline. Peter could unmistakably see that the Lord was in it all. To love God is to serve Him. How often God places before us opportunities to practice real Christlikeness! How often He makes our lessons spring to life.

A church building in Europe was bombed during World War II. In the explosion, a statue of Jesus was damaged—the hands were blown off. The statue has not been restored but remains with missing hands. Beneath the statue of Jesus these words are now engraved: "Christ has no hands but yours!"

God awaits a response to God-given opportunities. "Then Peter invited the men into the house to be his guests" (v. 23). These men had walked more than 30 miles. Peter invited these Gentiles to be his special guests—a big first step, coming from his background. Legalism would protest, "I have *never* done this before!" The language of liberty in Christ rejoices, "I have never done this *before!*"

What a fantastic picture! Inside the house of an outcast tanner, the apostle of Jesus hosts two Gentile servants and a Roman soldier—all residing together in fellowship. The Spirit of God was bringing them together, breaking down barriers, sweeping out prejudices, and opening doors to a whole new era in the Church of Jesus Christ.

The Spirit of love draws believers together. The angel in one of Thornton Wilder's plays says, "In Love's service only the wounded soldiers can serve."

Edwin Markham trusted a banker with the settlement of an estate. As a result, the banker betrayed him and left him penniless. Markham became bitter and ceased being productive as a poet.

One day, thinking and doodling with his pen, Markham found himself drawing circles. Making a large circle, he thought about how God's great circle of love takes us in—though undeserving! As his mind tried to grasp God's great love, inspiration hit him once again—after several years of deep resentment and bitterness. He began to write these familiar words:

> He drew a circle that shut me out—
> Heretic, rebel, a thing to flout!
> But Love and I had the wit to win;
> We drew a circle that took him in.

Love reached across the gulf of hatred; forgiveness showered that banker. The joy of the Lord flowed through Markham and once again he was able to write. Some of his greatest works followed.

God would have His people reach out to love across barriers, forgiving, helping, encouraging, lifting. He promises to give opportunities for unlimited love.

An old physician told a friend, "I've been practicing medicine for 30 years, and I have prescribed many things. But I have learned that for most of what ails people, the best medicine is love."

The friend asked skeptically, "But what if it doesn't work?"

He replied, "Double the dose!"

CHAPTER 6

"Fill My Cup, Lord!"

Acts 10:23-48

Have you read the episodes in the Book of Acts about the filling of the Holy Spirit and down deep inside wished somehow that could happen to you today? Have you stumbled or come up against something in your Christian walk and wondered, Is this all there is to it? Does the vigorous life in the New Testament Church leave you wondering if you have received all that God has for you?

In Caesarea, Cornelius the centurion was devoted to God and eager to possess all God had for him. Even though his good deeds and prayer life had been exemplary, he felt a sense of incompleteness. Behind the scenes, God was preparing Peter to come and tell Cornelius much more. Peter and 6 Jewish Christians traveled with 2 servants and a Roman guard sent from Cornelius. The 10 men arrived in Caesarea from Joppa the next day.

Along with a houseful of family and friends, Cornelius received Peter to hear his message. To the amazement of Peter's Jewish friends, the Holy Spirit suddenly fell on that crowd of Gentiles—just as He had come to the Jews at Pentecost eight years previously. The descent of God's Spirit upon the Gentiles signaled that God is no respecter of persons. When God's Spirit cleanses the heart by faith, no one—Jew or Gentile—is second class or "unclean."

In Acts 2, the Holy Spirit had filled the Jews at Pentecost; in Acts 8, the Samaritans—Jewish half-breeds; and now the Gentiles in Acts 10. Clovis Chappell once wrote:

> I have attended services that left me with a feeling that they had been utter failures. When the benediction was pronounced the people as they went away did not give the impression that they had been in green pastures beside still waters. They rather seemed to have been trudging through a desert or spending an hour in a dentist's chair. . . . But this service [in Acts 10] was a success. Those present were helped and inspired . . . transformed. . . . Not one who was present that day ever forgot this service. They spoke of it years afterward with glad and grateful tears. Yet it was a service that belongs no more to a far-off yesterday than it belongs to today.[1]

That wonderful service in Cornelius' house is more than an epic; it is an example. The Holy Spirit awaits to fall upon yielded hearts. For centuries the church made the mistake of believing Pentecost was a miracle never to be repeated. If one would lay aside the unique epochal manifestations and begin to pray for the Holy Spirit to fill him, he would have his own version of Pentecost—a revival fire right in his own city or church!

> *What I give, He takes;*
> *What He takes, He cleanses;*
> *What He cleanses, He fills;*
> *What He fills, He uses!*

Learning from Cornelius' experience, one can get some answers to the question, "How can I receive all that God has for me?"

One Needs a Strong Sense of Obedience

"As Peter entered the house, Cornelius met him and fell at his feet in reverence" (v. 25). Eastern custom gave honor and respect by kneeling down before someone highly regarded.

"But Peter made him get up. 'Stand up,' he said, 'I am only a man myself'" (v. 26). Peter's response showed the change in his thinking—Cornelius was an equal in God's sight. In spite of Peter's learned background of racial superiority, his immediate behavior recognized the manhood of Cornelius. God had indeed transformed Peter's heart and mind. The lesson of Peter's vision was now being put into practice. Peter commented, "But God has shown me that I should not call any man impure or unclean. So when I was sent for, I came without raising any objection. May I ask why you sent for me?" (vv. 28-29).

Cornelius told of his own angelic vision giving instructions to send for Peter. Cornelius added, "So I sent for you immediately" (v. 33). Everything about that Roman soldier shows his posture of obedience to the Lord. He was accustomed to giving orders and expecting immediate obedience. And he was accustomed to receiving orders from military superiors and giving immediate obedience. God never intimidated Cornelius into obedience. Loving God, he obeyed without question, without hesitation, instantly. What a great spiritual asset! "So I sent for you immediately."

Praying John Hyde said, "I know but one word—obedience. I know how a soldier will obey an order even unto death. I can't expect to look Jesus in the face and obey Him less than a soldier his commander."

Samuel said to King Saul, "To obey is better than sacrifice, and to heed is better than the fat of rams" (1 Sam. 15:22). Francis de Sales wrote, "Doing the little things with a strong desire to please God makes them really and truly great."

Obedience is a beautiful gift to offer the Lord, for in giving obedience one gives himself.

John T. Seamands powerfully illustrated this vital area of life:

> In Arabia, certain horses are trained especially for the service of the king. The primary lesson is that of obedience. For example, whenever the trainer blows his whistle in a certain way, the horses must learn to run toward him. The training goes on for months, and then a very interesting test is given.
>
> For several days the horses are deprived of water, until they become frantic with thirst and pace excitedly around the fenced-in area. Then suddenly the gate leading to the pond is opened, and the horses rush toward the water to quench their thirst. But just as they are about to drink, the trainer blows his whistle. The horses instinctively stop where they are. A tremendous struggle goes on within them. There is the maddening desire to stoop and drink, but their wills have been trained to obey the sound of the whistle. Those horses which turn away from the water at this criticial moment and run back to the trainer are the only ones considered fit for the service of the king.
>
> In like manner, those children of God who have learned to be sensitive to the leadings of the Spirit and to obey the will of the Father at all times are the only ones fit for the service of the King of Kings.[2]

Spiritual success comes by seeking and knowing, loving and obeying God. If one seeks, he will know. If one knows, he will love. And if one loves, he will obey.

One Needs a Strong Sense of Expectancy

Looking for God's wholeness, Cornelius leaned forward with anticipation: "Cornelius was expecting them and had called together his relatives and close friends" (v. 24). The verb "was expecting" or "was waiting" suggests an eager hope, one directing his mind toward something. He was

71

looking forward to whatever God had in mind. This kind of expectant hope is the dream of a man wide-awake!

An ex-soldier said, "During my time in a prisoner-of-war camp I came to realize the importance of hope. Hope was what sustained us; we expected little from the present but a great deal from the future!" And the posture of expectancy keeps one keenly aware that God is at work.

Expectancy was the climate of those people thronging narrow lanes and roadsides when Jesus was about to pass by. Watching the horizon, they wondered, "Will Jesus turn and look on me? Will He speak to me? Will I get to tell Him my problem and find help and healing for my need?"

Convinced something was about to happen, Cornelius called his family and special friends. What a beautiful demonstration of faith! It never occurred to him to doubt the angel's promise. To a person with a strong sense of expectancy, all doors have handles and hinges. To the doubtful and fearful, all doors have locks and latches.

When Peter came to preach, Cornelius and his crowd weren't smothering ho hums! They had been living and praying for God's best in their lives. Cornelius was eager to learn what God was going to do. He had prayed for more light— and God was faithful to give him more light.

Such expectancy creates enthusiasm. The only church which enjoys dead, solemn services is the one already dead! If one doesn't expect God to do much in his soul, he probably won't be disappointed.

A little Episcopalian girl visited her aunt's country Methodist church. After the Sunday morning service, the aunt asked, "What do you think of our minister?"

"Wonderful," she replied, "but our minister could preach good too if our choir would root for him like your choir does for your preacher!"

How long has your heart yearned for all that God has for you? Is your obedience up-to-date? Are you expecting God to hear your cry of silent desperation? Jesus says, "If you then, though you are evil, know how to give good gifts to your children, how much more will your Father in heaven give the Holy Spirit to those who ask him!" (Luke 11:13).

The songwriter catches the note of expectancy:

I just feel like something good is about to happen.
I just feel like something good is on its way.
He has promised that He'd open all of heaven,
And, brother, it could happen any day!

When God's people humble themselves to call on Jesus,
And they look to heaven expecting as they pray,
I just feel like something good is about to happen,
And, brother, this could be that very day!

I have learned in all that happens just to praise Him,
For I know He's working all things for my good;
Every tear I shed is worth all the investment,
For I know He'll see me through, He said He would.

He has promised eye nor ear can hardly fathom
All the things He has in store for those who pray.
I just feel like something good is about to happen,
*And, brother, this could be that very day!**

—Wm. J. Gaither

One Needs a Strong Sense of Openness

After thanking Peter for coming to his home, Cornelius said, "Now we are all here in the presence of God to listen to everything the Lord has commanded you to tell us" (v. 33). An attitude of openness pervaded the atmosphere.

"Now" is the special moment for them. All things have come about to provide this one great encounter with living truth. Cornelius said, "We are all here." No one had stayed away. No one wished to be left out of whatever God planned for them.

---

*© Copyright 1974 by Wm. J. Gaither. International copyright secured. All rights reserved. Used by special permission.

73

If one really longs to have God's best for his life, he should be where God's people meet—and when they meet. In the New Testament the filling of the Holy Spirit came upon gathered Christians. If one desires to receive the Holy Spirit in His fullness, filling heart and life, he ought to go where the action is. As Uncle Bud Robinson was quoted as saying, "I'd stay by the spout where the glory comes out!"

Who can forget that first Easter Sunday night when the resurrected Jesus appeared suddenly in the room with His disciples? Though fear had locked their doors, Jesus was with them, saying, "Receive the Holy Spirit" (John 20:22). In that joyful moment stands the disturbing note: "Thomas . . . was not with the disciples when Jesus came" (v. 24). He missed the sunrise of hope! For a whole week Thomas was buried under his unresolved doubt. If only he had not forsaken the gathering together, he would have experienced the presence of the living Christ!

Openness to God's truth includes putting oneself where God's truth is shared and proclaimed. One isn't much of a candidate for the Spirit's filling if one neglects the means of spiritual instruction and worship.

One fellow excused his frequent absences from church services by saying, "I could not be with you Sunday, but I was with you in spirit."

His pastor finally remarked, "Brother, I think spirits are a bit like dogs. If you can't come along to look after them, you had better keep them at home!"

Cornelius said, "Now we are all here in the *presence of God!*" It is not being together, but being together in God's presence that makes the difference. We never will find our way into the "secret place of the most High" (Ps. 91:1, KJV) on flippant and irreverent feet. We must be open books before God.

One needs to ask himself, "Am I open to God's truth?" Most of us at one time or another have sat in a classroom getting credit for being present when our minds were elsewhere—or, at best, skimming the surface. My wife and I were enrolled in a large English literature class during our college days. The professor was a good man—but not very interesting. Many times he would put on his glasses and read poetry or romantic literature. His droning voice and selection of material evoked about as much applause as a caterpillar romping over a carpet. Unfortunately, while reading with his glasses on, he couldn't see the students slipping out every possible exit—including windows! Some of us remained in class to finish homework for the next hour's class. Frankly, we weren't very open to his teaching.

However, Cornelius and his crowd were present before God. God knows our hearts and actions. He sees our willingness to listen and obey. God knows if we are here "to listen to everything the Lord has commanded" (v. 33).

Cornelius wasn't interested in Peter's opinion about Roman or Jewish law. He didn't invite Peter to debate. He wanted answers, not problems; certainties, not speculations, no guesswork, no hearsay, no theological puzzles, but "Thus saith the Lord"! Those people came to hear a word from the Lord. Cornelius wished to get his orders from the Commander in Chief. He, his family, and his friends were open to receive, to believe, and to obey!

Peter launched into his sermon. Since speaking to Gentiles without background in the Old Testament, he didn't quote it. Simply, but powerfully, Peter preached Christ— Christ crucified for our sins and Christ resurrected for our new life. The Bible says, "That which . . . we have heard, which we have seen with our eyes, which we have looked at and our hands have touched—this we proclaim concerning the Word of life" (1 John 1:1). The apostles spoke firsthand! Peter emphasized Jesus as "Lord of all" (v. 36).

The people drank in the good news about Jesus. But Peter didn't get to finish his sermon: "While Peter was still speaking these words, the Holy Spirit came on all who heard the message. The circumcised believers who had come with Peter were astonished that the gift of the Holy Spirit had been poured out even on the Gentiles" (vv. 44-45).

If one has a strong sense of obedience, of expectancy, and of openness before the Lord, then he can expect God to keep His promise to fill him with His Spirit. When one admits his need, God bestows the power.

To be filled with God's Spirit, one must expect Him, desire Him, listen to Him, be open to Him, and love Him. The Holy Spirit will come in His fullness. Although God demands a whole heart, He accepts a broken one if He gets all the pieces. It is full surrender.

In spite of many sermons on the filling of the Holy Spirit, for many life has gone on just the same. I pray that God will open your heart to perceive that the Holy Spirit is God's greatest Gift to every believer. Jesus said, "I will ask the Father, and he will give you another Counselor to be with you forever—the Spirit of truth" (John 14:16-17). His is not an empty promise!

An old woman in Scotland lived in terrible poverty. Her neighbors knew her son had gone to America and become prosperous. They wondered why he let his mother exist in such poverty.

One day a concerned friend asked, "Doesn't your son ever send you any money?"

"No," the mother replied reluctantly. But in his defense, she added, "He does write me nice, long letters and sends me a pretty picture in almost every letter."

The friend asked, "Where are the pictures? May I see them?"

"Certainly," the old lady answered. She hobbled over to a shelf and took down the old family Bible. Between the pages lay the "pictures" her son had been sending from America through all the years.

What were they? Banknotes—each for a considerable amount! During all her time of need, of living like a pauper, she had lying in her Bible enough wealth to satisfy all her needs and wants. But in her ignorance, she had looked at them as pictures and kept them as reminders of her far-off son.

Many people treat their Bibles that way. God, through His redeeming love, has provided for and sent to each one the wonderful gift of His Holy Spirit. Too many folk have left Him as an unclaimed promise in their closed Bibles. If one's spirit hungers and thirsts in spiritual poverty, he may be filled! If one is obedient to Him, expecting God's best, and open to His truth, then he may "be filled with the Spirit" (Eph. 5:18).

This sincere prayer expresses it beautifully:

Fill my cup, Lord, I lift it up, Lord!
Come and quench this thirsting of my soul;
Bread of heaven, feed me till I want no more.
*Fill my cup; fill it up and make me whole!**
　　　　　　　　　　—Richard Blanchard

CHAPTER 7

Baptized
with the Spirit
—Equipped to
Serve

Acts 11:1-18

The news traveled quickly: "Gentiles join the Church!" Expecting a victory rally upon his return to Jerusalem from Caesarea, Peter was surprised to find a protest rally. Hard-line legalists criticized him: "You went into the house of uncircumcised men and ate with them" (v. 3). More concerned for Peter's defilement than the Lord's work through him, they forgot Jesus had eaten with sinners and social rejects.

Peter's critics failed to distinguish between their unique religious system and the spirit of Christ! They had put codes of conduct in place of the music of praise. The Bible declares, "He has made us competent as ministers of a new covenant—not of the letter but of the Spirit; for the letter kills, but the Spirit gives life" (2 Cor. 3:6). From their Jewish background, it seemed right to pour new converts to Christ through the mold of Jewish laws. Little did they know that the gospel was breaking out of Judaism like a butterfly escaping its cocoon.

"Peter began and explained everything to them precisely as it had happened" (v. 4). Peter neither argued nor asserted his authority. Tracing the sequence of events, Cornelius' vision and his own, Peter reminded them he had taken six fellow Jewish believers with him to Caesarea.

William Barclay gave vivid insight:

> Together with himself that made seven persons present. In Egyptian law, which the Jews would know well, seven witnesses were necessary completely to prove a case. In Roman law, which they would also know well, seven seals were necessary to authenticate a really important document like a will. So Peter is in effect saying, "I am not arguing with you. I am telling you the facts and of these facts there are seven witnesses. The case is proved." The proof of Christianity always lies in facts. It is very doubtful if anyone has ever been argued into Christianity by verbal proofs and logical demonstrations. The proof of Christianity is that it works, that it does bring to men the Spirit of God; and therefore the duty of the Christian is not to talk about his faith but to demonstrate his faith. It is when a man's deeds give the lie to his words that the gravest discredit is brought on Christianity; it is when a man's words are guaranteed by his deeds that the world is presented with an argument for Christianity which will brook no denial.[1]

Peter doesn't claim to have a hot line to the mind of God. With the confidence of a man who knows he's right, he gave the facts of what had happened in Cornelius' house: "As I began to speak, the Holy Spirit came on them as he had come on us at the beginning" (v. 15). Peter's defense was not based on what he said, but upon what God did!

In welcoming Gentiles into the Church of Jesus Christ, Peter did not act alone and apart from other believers. He and the six other witnesses acted in harmony with God's actions. Peter was not a one-man church running off on his lone tangent.

Peter allowed Jesus' words to be his guide: "Then I remembered what the Lord had said, 'John baptized with water, but you will be baptized with the Holy Spirit.' So if God gave them the same gift as he gave us, who believed in the Lord Jesus Christ, who was I to think that I could oppose God!" (vv. 16-17). One preacher said it well: "The Scriptures are our 'check' for the leading of the Spirit. . . . We are not left to wonder whether or not . . . the Spirit [is] prompting us. . . . He gives us the Bible to test whether or not it is His leading. Unless confirmed in, by and through Scriptures, we can doubt that the 'feelings' . . . are truly Spirit-inspired."[2]

As the Holy Spirit came upon Cornelius and his close circle of influence, the Holy Spirit brought to Peter's mind something Jesus had said earlier: "John baptized with water, but you will be baptized with the Holy Spirit." Suddenly Peter saw the act of baptism, being submerged in water, as a graphic metaphor of the believer saturated with, submerged in, baptized with God's Spirit. It is not a literal statement of God's work, but a descriptive metaphor of how God works! Peter saw water baptism as merely the symbol or picture of God's spiritual baptism in our hearts.

Without putting too much evidence on the language of metaphor, there is an obvious difference between birth and baptism. In grace as in nature, birth precedes baptism. A sinner becomes a candidate for baptism with water after his new birth. It is by repentance. A believer is a candidate for baptism with the Spirit by his responsiveness. When he yields himself fully to God, God's Spirit will be given fully to him.

The filling of the Holy Spirit is described by various terms: entire sanctification, fullness of the Spirit, the deeper work, a second work of grace, and baptism with the Spirit. Some groups get hung up on one set of terms while others insist on another set of terms. All vocabularies are incomplete attempts to describe God's gift of the Holy Spirit residing in us and presiding in us—a reality beyond description. If one has trouble with the vocabulary of the metaphor of baptism, he should use whatever description helps him experience and appreciate the wonder of God's cleansing and empowering by the Spirit.

A cattleman in Texas had been converted to Christ. He was hungry for God's cleansing power in his heart. Attending a holiness camp meeting, he heard several sermons that whetted his appetite for God's fullness. However, he admitted to the preacher his prejudice against the terminology of "sanctification." He had witnessed inconsistencies in someone claiming to be "sanctified."

The evangelist asked the old cattleman, "What kind of pipes do you put in the ground to bring water to your cattle? Iron or galvanized?"

The cattleman replied, "Galvanized—iron would rust out soon."

The evangelist advised, "Brother, let's get down on our knees and ask God to galvanize you so your experience won't rust out!"

In his spiritual hunger and honest openness, the old rancher prayed that God would "galvanize" him. The Lord filled him with His overflowing Spirit. The man claimed God's great promise!

Water baptism is the outward identification with Christ. ✓ Baptism with the Spirit is the inner equipping for service. The metaphor of baptism with the Spirit suggests several things.

When Baptized with the Spirit, the Believer Is Immersed in the Spirit for Protection

Not only is God's Spirit in us, but He surrounds us and engulfs us. Like little fish swimming in the sea, the believer is immersed in the ocean of God's love. He can move with zest and joy in the atmosphere of God's Spirit: "For in him we live and move and have our being" (Acts 17:28).

Jesus' invitation to experience the new birth is described by one gospel song:

> *If you are tired of the load of your sin,*
> *Let Jesus come into your heart.*
> *If you desire a new life to begin,*
> *Let Jesus come into your heart.*
>
> *Just now, your doubtings give o'er.*
> *Just now, reject Him no more.*
> *Just now, throw open the door;*
> *Let Jesus come into your heart.*
> —Lelia N. Morris

"That is salvation," says W. A. Criswell, "letting Jesus come into your heart. But by Spirit baptism, the believer is placed 'in Christ.' Gal. 3:27 reads: 'For as many of you as have been baptized into Christ have put on Christ.' . . . We are in Christ as we are in our clothes. We are clothed in Christ. Spirit baptism places us there."[3] John 14:20 shows the difference between our spiritual birth and our spiritual baptism. In speaking of the coming of the Holy Spirit, Jesus said, "On that day you will realize that I am in my Father, and you are in me, and I am in you." The new birth is "I am in you." The baptism with the Spirit is "You are in me."

When Baptized with the Spirit, the Believer Is Cleansed by the Spirit for Purity

Baptism with water symbolizes the washing away of one's acts of sin. Baptism with the Spirit suggests the washing away of one's sin nature. It is God's promise of a clean heart. To be baptized with the Holy Spirit is to be purified in heart.

Years later Peter spoke of this same incident in Cornelius' house: "Brothers, you know that some time ago God made a choice among you that the Gentiles might hear from my lips the message of the gospel and believe. God, who knows the heart, showed that he accepted them by giving the Holy Spirit to them, just as he did to us. He made no distinction between us and them, for he purified their hearts by faith" (Acts 15:7-9).

Vegetables in a garden grow better when they aren't retarded and choked by weeds. Someone needs to clean out the weeds. A child develops more rapidly when his body isn't choked with disease. Someone needs to purge away disease. The soul matures more readily when the sin nature has been cleansed away. And God has promised to purify our hearts by faith.

A four-year-old boy was very shy toward soap and water. Saturday night came, and he put up his usual series of arguments about why he should not have to take a bath.

As his mother half-pulled him to the bathtub, she asked, "You want to be clean, don't you?"

"Yes," he sobbed, "but why can't you just dust me off like you do the furniture?"

A lot of Christians would rather be dusted off than cleansed by the Holy Spirit. They are only halfhearted about pure hearts and pure lives. But the Bible is a holy Book about a holy God who insists on a holy people. Therefore, He sent His holy Son who "loved the church and gave himself up for her to make her holy, cleansing her by the washing with water through the word, and to present her to himself as a radiant church, without stain or wrinkle or any other blemish, but holy and blameless" (Eph. 5:25-27).

God alone can cleanse our hearts by filling us, by immersing us, by saturating us with His Spirit!

When Baptized with the Spirit, the Believer Receives the Inner Work of the Spirit for Power

Water baptism symbolizes God's inner work of imparting new life. Baptism with the Spirit is evidence that our inner life has been yielded to Him. He baptizes us in response to our yieldedness. The old nature is dead and buried with Christ. Our new nature is alive unto God. This baptism with the Spirit results in power. Jesus promised, "But you will receive power when the Holy Spirit comes on you" (Acts 1:8). Those were His last parting words to His disciples before ascending into heaven. Jesus wanted it fresh on their minds. He promised that the Spirit's baptism would be their source of power. He gives the power to be Christlike.

It is not your power or mine—but His power. He has the power and we have Him: "The one who is in you is greater than the one who is in the world" (1 John 4:4).

When Baptized with the Spirit, the Believer Is Initiated into the Spirit for Performance

Water baptism is properly a visible initiation into God's kingdom for a public witness. The metaphor of baptism with the Spirit carries the idea of an initiation into the Spirit-controlled life of service. God does not intend for us to bask in the luxury of the Spirit's power. We receive His power to equip us for service. When He baptizes us we are fitted for ministry!

The question is often asked, "When do we get the Holy Spirit?" John T. Seamands responds: "When we are converted, we *have* the Holy Spirit—*all* of the Holy Spirit that we will ever have. So to be baptized or filled with the Spirit certainly does *not* mean that we get *more* of the Spirit; rather, the Holy Spirit gets *more of us*. For though we have all of the Spirit, He does not have all of us. He must have uncontested control of our lives, so that He does not simply dwell in us, but dwells unhindered . . . in all His fullness."[4]

There's a precious fullness of the Spirit known only to those surrendered totally to Him!

Several years ago I was invited to preach at a revival meeting in the Northwest. It was the first meeting in a beautiful new church building. The sanctuary and pastor's study were very attractive. The parsonage nearby had huge picture windows framing a spectacular view of Mount Hood on one side and Mount Adams on the other side. Entering the parsonage, I was given a tour of the house, introduced to the family, and taken to my room with a private shower. The gracious pastor said, "You can do anything here but kiss the cook!" For that week I was treated as a special guest. And it was a glorious week uniquely anointed by God!

Several years later that fine pastor moved to another church. The church board invited me to come, not as a guest, but as pastor. They were willing to turn the keys over to me. Where I once resided as guest, I would then preside as head of the house. Same man, same house—but the entire relationship would have been different!

Being baptized or filled with the Spirit is not a question of space—is He inside me or outside me? It is relational. It is turning all the keys over to Him! As Dr. William Greathouse wrote, "The key to every secret closet where our fondest treasures are hid. The key to the attic of our imaginations. The key to the basement of our desires. The Spirit enters to possess the entire personality. He may rearrange the furniture of our lives as He chooses. He has come to *dwell* within. . . . To yield ourselves up to Him in this way is to be *filled* with the Spirit."[5]

> *For mighty works for Thee, prepare*
> *And strengthen ev'ry heart.*
> *Come, take possession of Thine own,*
> *And nevermore depart.*
> —Charlotte G. Homer

As a believer, how may one receive the baptism of the Holy Spirit?

First, one must acknowledge his need for the Holy Spirit. Without Him one can do nothing!

Second, one must admit that the Holy Spirit is God's promised provision for the believer: "The promise is for you and your children and for all who are far off—for all whom the Lord our God will call" (Acts 2:39).

Third, one must accept God's gift by faith. Unlike Pentecost, one doesn't have to "tarry until . . ." One need not wait for the Spirit to come; He is already available to the born-again Christian. He waits for the opportunity to fill the open, yielded heart. "According to your faith be it unto you" (Matt. 9:29, KJV).

Uncle Bud Robinson, evangelist, was preaching on being filled with the Spirit. A woman came to pray. She struggled in prayer for the Lord to sanctify her, to fill her with His Spirit.

Stepping over to where she was praying and struggling at the altar, Uncle Bud touched her on the head. When she looked up, he said, "Woman, the last time I heard from heaven, God was taking every woman He could get!"

She threw up her hands and said, "Praise the Lord, that includes me!"

Jesus said, "If ye then, being evil, know how to give good gifts unto your children: how much more shall your heavenly Father give the Holy Spirit to them that ask him?" (Luke 11:13, KJV).

CHAPTER 8

Are You Christlike?

Acts 11:19-30

If we get courage, sometimes we ask, "Are you a Christian?" What if we phrased the question with the original meaning of the word Christian: "Are you Christlike?"

That's different. It's not just a label but the quality of likeness to Christ. The question is not, "Have you become a Christian?" The question addressed to the believer is, "Are you Christlike?" How are you getting along spiritually these days? Many could reply, "A sinner saved by grace so many weeks, months, or years ago!" That's great, fine; praise the Lord! But today, "Are you Christlike?"

Inconspicuously, Luke noted, "The disciples were first called Christians at Antioch" (v. 26). At first glance, it seems like a footnote casually dropped into the action. It turns out to be the hook upon which the whole passage hangs.

Luke resumed his narrative of the spread of Christianity: "Now those who had been scattered by the persecution in connection with Stephen traveled as far as Phoenicia, Cyprus and Antioch, telling the message only to Jews" (v. 19). What had been intended to stamp out the Church only scattered it. Persecuted in one city, believers fled to another—carrying their faith with them. New life sprang up everywhere!

In his narration, Luke focuses on the new life springing up in the city of Antioch. With a population of more than 600,000, Antioch was the third main city of the Western world. Only Rome and Alexandria, Egypt, were more influential. Antioch was a busy northern capital, a commercial center where European and Asian cultures collided. Here Greek culture touched the Syrian desert in a social melting pot. Differences did not seem so important here as they did in isolated, provincial, religious Jerusalem.

A sports center, Antioch specialized in chariot races. Five miles outside the city stood the temple of Daphne where Apollo and Artemis were worshiped in passionate sexual orgies with religious prostitutes. With its university and centers for art and science, Antioch throbbed with man's quest for knowledge and expression.

The big city became ripe soil for the gospel of Jesus Christ. Cities have a way of magnifying the best and worst in human nature.

In that first century, cities became targets for spreading the gospel. In fact, Antioch soon became headquarters for the Gentile church, quickly passing Jerusalem as center for the Christian faith. The apostle Paul would soon make Antioch his base of operations.

The people of Antioch developed a caustic wit, a Don Rickles style of humor which jeered and called names. Well known for their mockery and sarcasm, these masters of ridicule lampooned actors and emperors alike.

Some unknown punster coined the slang word "Christian." Antioch laughingly took it up as the best word to deride the believers of "Christus." Originally, "Christian" was good for big laughs at Antioch.[1]

Names have a way of sticking. When Captain Cook discovered Australia, his sailors brought aboard a strange-looking animal. Not knowing what it was, Captain Cook sent a sailor to ask the natives what was the animal's name. Upon his return, he reported it was known as a "kangaroo."

Many years later, it was learned that when the natives responded with "kangaroo," they were simply asking, "What did you say?"

"The disciples were first called Christians at Antioch." Apparently believers talked about Christ—not the church. They were first-century "Jesus freaks"! Antioch laughed, "These fellows are Christlike!"

Perhaps the church resented it at first, for the word "Christian" is used only three times in the New Testament— twice in derision.

Though this name was given in reproach by enemies, one day disciples would glory in that name. A few generations later the Church would recite in its liturgy the prayer, "We thank Thee that the name of Thy Christ is named upon us, and so are we one with Thee."

It would become a badge of honor! One observed, "There was an unintended compliment behind Antioch's contempt. 'Christian' reveals what outsiders associated in their minds most with believers: Jesus Christ."[2]

Before conversion, people might be Jews or Gentiles, Greeks or Romans—but after conversion, they were called by one name: "I am Christian!"

"The disciples were first called Christians at Antioch." The Greek word for "were called" means literally "were doing business as" or "to transact business." It refers to giving a name to someone derived from his business. English family names often came from the family's trade or occupation, such as Miller, Baker, Carpenter, Smith, Cooper (one who makes barrels), Fletcher (one who makes arrows), Weaver, or Sawyer.

Apparently "Christians" were occupied with Christ. Working in the Christ-way seemed to outsiders as the main business of the disciples. The name Christian stuck because those enthusiastic disciples put Jesus first!

"Are you Christian?" Like coins, words get worn down by usage. When a coin has been used a lot, its first clear imprint from the mint gets dulled.

The word Christian has gotten dulled. It has been worn down by cultural meanings. For some it means "Western culture." For others it suggests "American" or a religious institution or a certain cultural life-style or vocabulary.

Going back to its first clear-cut, fresh image of Jesus, let me ask, "Are you Christlike?"

What qualities in the believers in Antioch reminded onlookers of Jesus Christ? At least five qualities are implied.

Like Christ, They Had a Personal Interest

"Some of them, however, men from Cyprus and Cyrene, went to Antioch and began to speak to Greeks also, telling them the good news about the Lord Jesus" (v. 20).

A few daring fellows began telling individuals about Jesus. It mattered not to them if people were Jew or Greek or Californian. They saw each person as one for whom Christ died. Each one was included in Jesus' invitation for new life—eternal life. Swaddling clothes of Jewish sectarianism were stripped off. God's love expressed through Jesus Christ was for anyone.

Jesus was like that, too. He reached out for anyone—regardless of race or class. These disciples in Antioch were cut from His pattern. They were interested in people—individuals.

Are you Christlike? Do you have a personal interest in people?

Like Christ, They Had a Divine Touch

"The Lord's hand was with them, and a great number of people believed and turned to the Lord" (v. 21).

90

"The Lord's hand" is a Semitic metaphor describing God's power. It suggests the Spirit of God. His Spirit works through God's man or woman, touching hearts of those around them. Without His divine touch, nothing of consequence would happen.

The touch of God was evident in changed lives. There was more to their testimonies and prayers and preaching than human display or effort. God blessed them. God was at work through them.

Antioch Christians resembled Jesus, who had God's obvious blessing. God's anointing on His life brought healing and help to others. The divine touch is not a luxury to apply to ourselves. That wonderful, effective touch of God through us changes broken lives!

One man harbored hostility toward the church. As he passed by the building where the church met, he threw rocks at it. One day something in the singing caught his attention. For the first time he entered and heard the story of Jesus.

It changed his life. His hostility was gone. Hungering to know more about Jesus, he got a Bible and began to read it. The more he read God's promises, the more his heart was thrilled. Sometimes he couldn't contain his joy. He would run outside and read a verse of Scripture to the first person he met on the street: "Have you heard about this?" Those who had known him recognized God's touch on his life.

Are you Christlike? Does anyone sense God's touch upon your life?

Like Christ, They Had a Shared Grace

"News of this reached the ears of the church at Jerusalem, and they sent Barnabas to Antioch. When he arrived and saw the evidence of the grace of God, he was glad and encouraged them all to remain true to the Lord with all their hearts" (vv. 22-23).

Luke says the Jerusalem church "sent" Barnabas to Antioch. The word, *exapostello*, means "to send out," coming from the same root as "apostle." Perhaps leaders in Jerusalem deputized Barnabas as their apostle to Antioch. Arriving in that busy city and locating the church, Barnabas "saw the evidence of the grace of God."

Stedman asks:

> Now how do you see grace? Grace means the goodness of God poured out into a life—an invisible quality. How do you see that?
>
> The word for grace here is the same word that the Apostle Paul employs in speaking about the gifts of the Holy Spirit: "But grace was given to each of us according to the measure of Christ's gift" (Eph. 4:7).
>
> In other words, grace is a gift of the Spirit, such as ... wisdom, knowledge, faith, discernment, prophecy, teaching and so forth. When Barnabas saw the gifts of the Holy Spirit at work he knew that these people were real Christians.[3]

The Bible says, "This salvation, which was first announced by the Lord, was confirmed to us by those who heard him. God also testified to it by signs, wonders, and various miracles, and gifts of the Holy Spirit distributed according to his will" (Heb. 2:3-4).

God's grace was seen in the equipping ministry of spiritual gifts. God equips His Church to produce Christlike character and Christlike service.

We are the supporting cast; Jesus is the Star! Our praying, serving, seeking, loving, and caring are for His glory. By God's design, we are dependent upon one another, working together as God has assigned, sharing His love in action. We can neither select nor glory in whatever gifts of the Spirit He has distributed to us.

Jesus Christ embodied all the gifts—and as Christ's Body, we shall exercise the same graces. Is there any *needed* service lacking in one's church fellowship? If so, it is either not a spiritual church of real disciples, or someone is refusing to use the gift God has equipped him with!

Are you Christlike?

Like Christ, They Had a Redemptive Fellowship

In describing Barnabas, Luke wrote, "He was a good man, full of the Holy Spirit and faith, and a great number of people were brought to the Lord.

"Then Barnabas went to Tarsus to look for Saul, and when he found him, he brought him to Antioch. So for a whole year Barnabas and Saul met with the church and taught great numbers of people. The disciples were first called Christians at Antioch" (vv. 24-26).

In nothing did those people become more Christian or Christlike than in their redemptive fellowship. Barnabas and the church at Antioch willingly brought Saul of Tarsus into their fellowship. That's the same young man who had torn up the church and then, after his conversion, had failed to exercise complete wisdom. In his misguided zeal, Saul had to be shelved, set aside, and put on "Hold."

Good old Barnabas had a heart of gold. And he had a church willing to take a risk on Saul. To me this is the most beautiful quality of the Antioch church—the willingness to be a redemptive fellowship. It is no accident that Luke slipped in the note right here: "The disciples were first called Christians at Antioch."

Without that quality, they could not be Christlike.

When Saul had come fresh from his conversion in Damascus, believers in Jerusalem were afraid of him. The tormentor had returned! But Barnabas believed in Saul and welcomed him into the fellowship. Now, after 10 or 12 years, Barnabas could still see possibilities in Saul—even when it looked like his future was bleak. Since Barnabas was filled with the Spirit of God, the fruit of love was evidenced by joy, long-suffering, patience, gentleness, and so on. He reached out for Saul, brought him to Antioch, and gave him opportunity to serve.

For a whole year, Barnabas and Saul kept busy helping new Christians. They "met with the church" (v. 26). The Greek word for "met with" could also mean, "They were entertained by the church." The same Greek word is used when Jesus said, "I was a stranger and you *invited* me in" (Matt. 25:35). The church "welcomed" Saul with his shaky past.

Sunlight filtered through stained-glass windows enhancing the beauty of the organ prelude. The congregation settled into an attitude of prayer. A woman, sitting with her husband and son, heard the floor of the center aisle creak softly. A latecomer paused at their pew looking for a place to sit. Obviously cleanliness was not one of his virtues—and he reeked with alcohol.

Just as the mother was hoping the man would spot a vacancy elsewhere, her little boy tugged at her arm. He whispered, "Mother, the man needs a place to sit!"

Suddenly she realized that while she had been concerned about an hour of discomfort, her son had seen a man in need. No doubt other needs had led that unkempt, confused man to church. The family moved over to make room as the boy called out, "Hey, mister, there's room here!"

The man turned unsteadily and sat down.

The mother admitted, "When we bowed our heads for prayer, I asked forgiveness. It had been easy to help those who were lovely. Now I prayed that I might have genuine concern for the unlovely."[4]

Can a fellow with a broken heart, a blotted past, a bad track record find from the fellowship of your church love, acceptance, and forgiveness? In the New Testament, the only ones Jesus condemned were those pretending to have no need! Jesus never made a man squirm over his past when he came asking for love, acceptance, and forgiveness.

Having experienced the joy of a redemptive fellowship, Paul later wrote: "Be kind and compassionate to one another,

94

forgiving each other, just as in Christ God forgave you" (Eph. 4:32).

Like Christ, They Had a Spontaneous Generosity

In verses 27 to 30, Luke tells of the great famine. From secular history as well as Josephus, Jewish historian, we know that Judea was especially hit hard. There's a beautiful response in the Antioch Christians: "The disciples, each according to his ability, decided to provide help for the brothers living in Judea" (v. 29).

Early in the Church, mercy to the poor and suffering began to blossom. It was incredible that citizens of Antioch would care for citizens in Jerusalem. But, in belonging to Christ, they belonged to each other. That was something new. Had not Jesus said, "All men will know that you are my disciples if you love one another" (John 13:35)? Having eternal life in common, it was natural to share the benefits of this life with brothers in need!

No doubt the church of Antioch included slaves, laborers, many people with not much money—but they shared, "each according to his ability."

Along with their money, they sent people—Barnabas and Saul. It's important to send money, but it takes people to ✓ translate money into godly love, compassion, and acts of kindness. The personal touch added the "plus" of love.

No adequate picture can ever be drawn of Christianity without its flowing, spontaneous, joyful generosity. And Jesus is always our Example of self-giving.

Jerry Cook related an incident portraying love in action:

A house in Portland's west hills burned down, and the man who lived there lost everything. He thought he was insured, but through some sort of slip-up, he was not, and he was wiped out financially.

The members of a nearby church, several of whom were carpenters and contractors, pitched in, took offerings, supplied labor, and totally rebuilt his house, without a penny coming out of his pocket. They did it simply because they felt the Lord wanted them to do it. The man was not even a member of their church.

Utterly overwhelmed by such a show of kindness, the man was solidly converted to Christ. The people who helped him had not done so because they planned to convert him that way. They helped him because he had a need and they had the capacity to meet that need. The impact on the neighborhood was profound. People still drive by to see the "house the Christians rebuilt!"[5]

Let me ask, "Are you Christlike?"

In our world today it is acceptable to call yourself a Christian. But it hungers for you to be Christlike!

A column of slaves was forced to march along a beach of West Africa. The Blacks moaned in their misery. One young man held himself with dignity. In spite of chains, bleeding welts, and curses from his captors, he remained erect. Someone noticed him—he was different. He acted with a certain grace. Another replied, "He cannot forget that he bears the name of the chief."

If you take the name Christian, don't forget that you bear the name of Christ. Are you Christlike?

Actor Hal Holbrook spent three and one-half hours getting into Mark Twain's makeup, but he had spent 13 years getting into Mark Twain's character.

A Christian might spend three and one-half hours preparing to talk about Christ, but it takes a lifetime to get into Christ's character! It is more than one act or one moment's decision. It is the surrender of a life, a willingness to learn and to be led by God's Spirit. Christlikeness is a way of life. May this be our prayer:

> *Have Thine own way, Lord! Have Thine own way!*
> *Hold o'er my being absolute sway!*
> *Fill with Thy Spirit till all shall see*
> *Christ only, always living in me!*
> —Adelaide A. Pollard

CHAPTER 9

Specializing in the Impossible

Acts 12:1-19

In Acts 12, Luke makes a significant transition. Two notable changes occur. First, in the life of the Church, Jerusalem passes into the wings. Antioch becomes the new center for Christianity. Second, Peter passes out of Luke's focus: "Then [Peter] left for another place" (v. 17). After Acts 12, Paul leads the evangelistic ministry of the Church for the next 20 years (A.D. 45-65).

Peter's third imprisonment and miraculous deliverance dramatically concluded one of the most picturesque careers in the Bible. When everything looked bleak, God made a way. When life seemed impossible, God gave deliverance. And still today, my God "is able to do immeasurably more than all we ask or imagine, according to his power that is at work within us" (Eph. 3:20).

If facing the seemingly impossible, one may bring it to the Lord. The character of a man's god determines the nature of his prayers. Peter's deliverance holds the keys of great release.

Trust Is the Key to Unanswered Questions

"It was about this time that King Herod arrested some who belonged to the church, intending to persecute them" (v. 1).

When the Communists took over Czechoslovakia, people were loaded into vans to be taken to detention camps. An old man realized his wife, being forced to leave her home and prized possessions, was about to break under the trauma. He said to her, "Hurry up! Let's not miss the van. The best people are already in jail; we must get there before they start taking just *anybody!*"

King Herod did not arrest "just anybody." He jailed "some who belonged to the church." Neutral, passive people are not persecuted!

Years ago, Christians in Korea faced persecution and imprisonment. Some not yet arrested complained to the missionary: "Maksa, something must be wrong in our Methodist church. Are we lacking in faith? Thirty-seven Presbyterians are in jail—and only one Methodist. I wonder if the Lord counts us worthy to suffer persecution?"

No one persecutes a person who does not matter. "[Herod] had James, the brother of John, put to death with the sword" (v. 2). James, the first martyred apostle, suffered under the first political persecution of the Church. In a whimsical move to appease the Jews, King Herod disposed of James as a pawn of political expediency. James was beheaded with a sword, an execution reserved for teachers accused of perverting the faith!

"When [Herod] saw that this pleased the Jews, he proceeded to seize Peter also. . . . So Peter was kept in prison" (vv. 3, 5). Why did God permit James to be executed and then deliver Peter? I've seen people die I knew we could not spare. I've asked, "What is God doing?" If God can deliver Peter, then why not James?

98

Life's unanswered questions must wait! God has not yet fully explained himself. The fact of evil baffles man's idea of "fairness." Some attempt to convince themselves that evil doesn't exist. Others surrender blindly to it.

During World War II many soldiers took a fatalistic attitude: "When my number is up, the bullet or bomb will get me."

One chaplain asked a young man, "But suppose you sat on the deck of a blacked-out ship and lighted a cigarette. Suppose the flicker of that light attracted the attention of an enemy submarine. If the sub torpedoed your ship, could you honestly say it was because your number is up?"

The young man admitted his own responsibility. Fatalism isn't a firm foundation. We have a Heavenly Father—not blind fate.

Stoics bear evil tearlessly. Cynics scoff at it. Christian Science denies evil. Buddhists endure it, hoping for personal extinction. Hindus accept evil as punishment for previous sin. Moslems fatalistically submit to it. But the Christian responds with trust! God did not abolish evil. He did not even stop the Crucifixion, but He brought Jesus through the Resurrection from death. Ultimately He defeated evil.

At times truth seems forever on the scaffold and wrong forever on the throne. Though we do not always have answers to our questions, we have assurance that God watches and cares, that His unseen hand is at the controls.[1]

Trust is not always a simple, easy response. However, trust is the only adequate response. With the fact of evil in our world, we might not always be *safe*, but as long as we trust God we shall always be *saved!* "For I am convinced that neither death nor life, neither angels nor demons, neither the present nor the future, nor any powers, neither height nor depth, nor anything else in all creation, will be able to separate us from the love of God that is in Christ Jesus our Lord" (Rom. 8:38-39).

The Bible teaches faith's triumph in the midst of suffering. God is worthy of our trust whether we understand our trials or not!

Prayer Is the Key to Impossible Situations

"So Peter was kept in prison, but the church was earnestly praying to God for him" (v. 5). The phrase "but the church" is a reversal of direction. Things looked impossible for Peter, "but the church" began to pray. Does prayer have a chance against a prison? Prayer reaches behind man-made walls and barriers. Luther said he would rather have an army against him than 100 people praying!

A teacher found two children down on their knees in the school corridor. Discovering they were gambling, she blurted out with relief, "Thank goodness! I thought at first you were praying!"

In an impossible situation, the church prayed "earnestly." More accurately, they prayed "with agony." Those groanings which cannot be uttered are often prayers which cannot be refused! One commented, "The people who pray effectively are the people who really care most. Prayer is not a discipline, a technique, or a method. It is primarily a concern, a motive, a desire. And so Christian love is basic in all our discoveries about prayer."[2]

William Law wrote, "There is nothing which makes us love a man so much as praying for him." To intercede means "to pass between." Intercessory prayer is love standing between God and man to draw them together.

"The night before Herod was to bring him to trial, Peter was sleeping between two soldiers, bound with two chains, and sentries stood guard at the entrance" (v. 6). According to Roman regulations, two guards were stationed outside in front of the gate and two just inside—an imposing display of military might! Herod must have remembered Peter's last imprisonment and escape, so he took no chances. He had Peter chained to two more Roman guards.

It didn't seem to bother Peter much: "Peter was sleeping." James was dead and Peter's turn would come in the morning. With clear conscience and total commitment to God's control, Peter rested secure in the Great Shepherd: "Yea, though I walk through the valley of the shadow of death, I will fear no evil: for thou art with me" (Ps. 23:4, KJV). Experiencing the peace Jesus gives, Peter slept so soundly the angel had to bump him to arouse him. It was peace, not after √ the storm, but in it!

"Suddenly an angel of the Lord appeared and a light shone in the cell. He struck Peter on the side and woke him up. 'Quick, get up!' he said, and the chains fell off Peter's wrists.

"Then the angel said to him, 'Put on your clothes and sandals.' And Peter did so" (vv. 7-8).

The angel thought about even the details of need— √ clothes and sandals. Nothing escapes God's attention as He cares for us with His great love!

Studying Acts 12, Dr. E. Stanley Jones noted the angel's attention to little needs. He bowed his head and asked, "Father, have You anything to say to me through this?"

"Yes," the Lord replied, "I'm looking after the details of your need."

Dr. Jones added, "As I walked out of the plane at San Francisco to change to another plane for Honolulu, there was my shaving kit which I had left in the washroom. Someone had picked it up and put it in the passageway. I picked it up, thanked the Father for looking after the details of need—a shaving kit, comparable to sandals and a coat."[3]

"'Wrap your cloak around you and follow me,' the angel told him. Peter followed him out of the prison . . . They passed the first and second guards and came to the iron gate

101

leading to the city. It opened for them by itself, and they went through it" (vv. 8-10).

In response to the church's prayers, God opened locked doors! When everything else fails, prayer gets results. The Lord began Peter's deliverance from that impossible situation even while the saints were praying. Devoid of political clout, the early Christians couldn't stay out of jail. Yet, endued with the power of the Holy Spirit, no prison could hold them! Charles Wesley's hymn captured the drama:

> Long my imprisoned spirit lay,
>   Fast bound in sin and nature's night.
> Thine eyes diffused a quick'ning ray.
>   I woke; the dungeon flamed with light.
> My chains fell off, my heart was free.
>   I rose, went forth, and followed Thee.

Prayer is our avenue to the impossible. God can set our spirits free. He gives release!

"When they had walked the length of one street, suddenly the angel left him" (v. 10). One noted, "The tides of inspiration come and go; the waves of divine energy flood and ebb; the angels appear and disappear. The parent goes so far with the child, and then the child must be prepared to go the rest of the way by himself. . . . When the angel departs, some people go to pieces; others keep right on going."[4] Once on the outside, Peter was left to his own common sense.

Charles Allen wrote: "Prayer is never a substitute for effort. A certain schoolboy failed in his examinations. He was very much surprised. When the teacher inquired how much he had studied, he replied, 'I did not study at all. I thought that if you asked God to help you, that was all you had to do.'"[5]

The man who asks God for a job should go looking for one. The farmer who prays for crops must plow and plant and cultivate. Prayer doesn't remove responsibility!

Dwight L. Moody was aboard ship when a fire broke out. A Christian friend urged Moody to pray. Moody responded, "I'm all prayed up! You pray; I'm going to pass the water buckets!" There's a time to pray and a time to work!

A fellow in Argentina worked in a bank which had gone on strike for 42 days. The banking system was a mess. No salaries were paid. The young man was supporting his mother, five sisters, and a little brother. Finally his money ran out.

He began to pray, "Lord, I have never actually experienced a true answer to prayer. Please show me one answer to prayer. Send me some money for bus fare to the bank. Send it in some way that shows me it came from You."

The next morning he got up early enough to walk to work in case no money came. In his mind, he thought the Lord would send someone to drop off a quarter for bus fare. No one came—so he started walking to the bus stop.

Each step he watched for money on the ground. At his bus stop, people were fumbling around with their change— but nothing for him.

He walked to the next bus stop. Arriving, he searched but found nothing. One more bus line to town was about eight blocks farther. Surely the quarter would be there!

After walking about three blocks in the darkness and fog, he heard someone trying to push a car out of a garage. The man huffed and puffed but couldn't push it out. The young man offered to help. Together they pushed and the car rolled down the hill, started up, and disappeared in the fog.

Continuing toward the last bus stop, he heard a car idling in the foggy darkness of early morning. It was the man whom he had helped. Opening his window, the stranger apologized for not offering a ride.

"Where are you going?" the driver asked. When the young man told him, he replied, "I work at the bank across the street from yours. I'd be happy to give you a ride!"

It had been a tremendous test for that young fellow—an important lesson. He had his first experience with God who hears and answers prayer.

"Then Peter came to himself and said, 'Now I know without a doubt that the Lord sent his angel and rescued me'" (v. 11). Up to this point, Peter thought it was a dream. Suddenly he grasped what had happened—God had rescued him from an impossible situation! Most often, in retrospect, we discern God's providence. Usually our hindsight is better than our foresight.

During the night, armies and chariots of the Arameans surrounded the mountain where Elisha and his servant slept. In the morning, the servant was horrified to see the enemy on every side: "Oh, my Lord, what shall we do?"

Elisha looked around and said, "Don't be afraid. . . . Those who are with us are more than those who are with them." Then Elisha prayed, "O Lord, open his eyes so he may see."

The Bible says, "Then the Lord opened the servant's eyes, and he looked and saw the hills full of horses and chariots of fire all around Elisha" (2 Kings 6:15-17). Just beyond our sight stand the hosts of the Lord! We are not left alone and unprotected.

A missionary and his wife traveled through dangerous territory occupied by cannibals belligerent toward white people. A late start and a breakdown of their jeep left them stranded in the dark night. The missionary set out on foot to find help, leaving his wife alone in the jeep. While he was gone several hours, she did a lot of praying. In fact, she prayed until she felt the presence of the Lord—and in that peace went to sleep.

Her husband returned at daybreak and awakened her. Near the jeep a lot of footprints circled around her. Strangely, however, the footprints came only so close to the stranded vehicle—and no closer! When the jeep was repaired, they went home safely.

Later, a spiritual breakthrough came to that territory. Many cannibals were converted to Jesus Christ. During the revival, one man testified of his conversion. He told what had made such an impression on him. One night he and his friends had come upon a jeep stranded in the dark. They intended to take the white woman as victim. As they approached the jeep, they saw huge, fiery guardians placed around that jeep—and the men fled in terror!

When people in desperate circumstances pray, God delivers completely. One cannot go by sight. We live in the age of faith—and God's hosts are standing by. The Bible says, "The angel of the Lord encamps around those who fear him, and he delivers them" (Ps. 34:7). Most of us only recognize God's hand of deliverance after the crisis is over! But prayer is the key to the impossible.

An unknown author wrote:

> I dreamed I was walking along the beach with the Lord, and across the sky flashed scenes from my life. For each scene I noticed two sets of footprints in the sand; one belonged to me, the other to the Lord. When the last scene of my life flashed before me I looked back at the footprints in the sand. I noticed that many times along the path of my life, there was only one set of footprints. I also noticed that it happened at the very lowest and saddest times in my life.
>
> I questioned the Lord about it. "Lord, You said that once I decided to follow You, You would walk with me all the way; but I have noticed that during the most troublesome times in my life, there is only one set of footprints. I don't understand why in times when I needed You most, You would leave."
>
> The Lord replied, "My precious child, I would never leave you during your times of trial and suffering. When you see only one set of footprints, it was then that I carried you."

Expectancy Is the Key to Paralyzing Doubt

"When this had dawned on him, he went to the house of Mary the mother of John, also called Mark, where many people had gathered and were praying" (v. 12).

The praying church gathered behind doors locked for fear and doubt. Though the devil may wall one in, he can't roof one in! Plagued with doubt, those Christians believed that God *could* deliver—but they didn't expect God to do it.

Perhaps they prayed that God would help Peter die with dignity. Maybe they prayed that Peter could leave a good witness to the guards. Too often Christians limit their prayers to whatever they think God will do. Apparently, as Ogilvie noted, "They believed more about the formidable power of man than they believed about the unlimited power of God. The prison and the guards—who could escape that? And look at James, he didn't escape. . . . We feel we must protect God's reputation by never getting out on a limb with requests which may not be granted. Our faith is so frail that we feel we cannot afford a disappointment which would snap the thin thread of our hope that He is real, that He hears and answers prayer."[6]

"Peter knocked at the outer entrance, and a servant girl named Rhoda came to answer the door. When she recognized Peter's voice, she was so overjoyed she ran back without opening it and exclaimed, 'Peter is at the door!'" (vv. 13-14).

Hearing a knock, Rhoda went "to answer"—a word describing the doorkeeper's responsibility to go to the door, to listen carefully if there might be more than one person, to ask who is there, and what is his business. At a time when Christians were being arrested, Rhoda performed her duty well at the sudden interruption of the prayer meeting.

Rhoda, whose name means "Rose," accepted the miracle without question. Delighted, she left Peter standing outside.

The group was shocked by her announcement: "Peter is at the door!"

"'You're out of your mind,' they told her. When she kept insisting that it was so, they said, 'It must be his angel'" (v. 15). Paralyzed by doubt, they did not expect God to answer so soon! At first they thought Rhoda was crazy—then, because she seemed so sincere, they rationalized, "It must be his angel." Why not? That seemed more believable—nobody was praying for his angel to appear! Popular superstitious folklore insisted each man has a guardian angel in his own likeness. Perhaps the ghost had come to inform of Peter's death!

This is one of the most comical scenes in the Bible. The group had gathered to pray for Peter languishing in jail. One would assume they prayed for his release. And now, their prayer meeting was interrupted: "Peter is standing outside!"

"Quiet! Can't you see we are busy praying for Peter in jail?"

"Yes—but Peter is here!"

"Please don't interrupt our prayer meeting. It is very important. We are urging God to do something for Peter!"

Farmers gathered with their families to pray for rain to end the terrible drought. Only one little girl brought an umbrella!

"But Peter kept on knocking" (v. 16). An iron prison gate, carefully guarded, is opened without hands—and Peter walked right through. But a simple house door which any girl could open remains locked. Peter couldn't get through. Unbelief keeps doors locked! Expectancy is the key to paralyzing doubt.

The doubting church expected nothing—so they kept on praying rather than open the gate to accept God's answer. They weren't ready for God's answer.

A congregation got concerned for their pastor. They began to pray, "Lord, revive him or remove him!" They were certain God would remove him. When God revived him, they couldn't handle it. "They found greater pleasure in the problem than assurance in the answer."[7]

A certain father prayed much for his son. He was deeply concerned over the young man's emotional problems. When he shared his burden with a friend, his friend said, "Unless you are willing to spend time with your son, all the praying will miss the mark! You are the answer to your own prayers. Your son needs *you!*"

The father refused to recognize the answer—so he kept right on praying for his son to change.[8]

God's answer may already be on its way. God's answer may be right around you. Expect God to hear above your doubts! Ask God to show you His answer.

In Schultz's cartoon strip, Lucy writes a note: "Dear Santa Claus, How have you been?" She stops to comment, "I feel like an idiot writing to someone who doesn't exist. On the other hand, if he really does exist and I don't write, I'd feel even dumber."

A companion replies, "This is the time of the year when it's best to touch all bases."

Could it be we often pray through our lack of expectation just to cover all the bases? One should expect God to hear and answer. Our world is never changed with question marks!

"And when they opened the door and saw him, they were astonished. Peter motioned with his hand for them to be quiet and described how the Lord had brought him out of prison. 'Tell James and the brothers about this,' he said, and then he left for another place" (vv. 16-17).

When the Christians finally opened the door and saw Peter, "They were astonished," ecstatic! Literally, "they stood out of themselves!" God had gone beyond their expectations. Isn't that just like Him?

Trust is the key to unanswered questions. Prayer is the

108

key to impossible situations. Expectancy is the key to paralyzing doubts.

When old King Herod couldn't find Peter, he cross-examined the guards and had them executed! But the empty prison remains an eloquent testimony to God's power.

In modern times, the chief lama of a Tibetan community arrested the Christian, Sundar Singh. He ordered Sundar thrown into a dry well and the lid securely locked. Sundar was left to die amid the rotting bones and decayed flesh of previous victims at the bottom of the well.

During the third night, Sundar cried to the Lord in prayer. Suddenly he heard the lid being unlocked and removed. A voice called down, "Grab the rope!" Since his arm had been injured in the fall, Sundar put his foot into a loop and hung on with one arm.

He was drawn up, the lid was replaced and locked. The cool, fresh air revived him, and his arm felt whole again. Looking around to thank his rescuer, no one was there.

At dawn, Sundar Singh returned to the village where he had been arrested and began preaching again. The news traveled to the lama.

Sundar was brought before him and questioned. Hearing the story of Sundar's rescue, the lama declared someone must have gotten the key and let him out. Somebody was a traitor! The search began for the key. It was found attached to the lama's own belt!

God mocks impossibilities!

> *Got any rivers you think are uncrossable?*
> *Got any mountains you can't tunnel through?*
> *God specializes in things thought impossible;*
> *And He can do what no other power can do.**
> —Oscar C. Eliason

Notes

CHAPTER 1

1. George Arthur Buttrick, ed., *The Interpreter's Bible* (New York: Abingdon Press, 1954), 9:120.
2. Source unknown.
3. Arnold E. Airhart, *Beacon Bible Expositions* (Kansas City: Beacon Hill Press of Kansas City, 1977), 5:103.
4. Henry Jacobsen, *The Acts Then and Now* (Wheaton, Ill.: Scripture Press Publications, 1973), 79-80.

CHAPTER 2

1. William E. McCumber, *Preaching Holiness from the Synoptic Gospels* (Kansas City: Beacon Hill Press of Kansas City, 1972), 93.
2. Bishop Festo Kivengere, *I Love Idi Amin* (Old Tappan, N.J.: Fleming H. Revell Co., 1977), 28.
3. Buttrick, *Interpreter's Bible*, 9:125.
4. Airhart, *BBE*, 106.
5. Haralan Popov, *Tortured for His Faith* (Grand Rapids: Zondervan Publishing House, 1972), 17-18.
6. Ray C. Stedman, *Birth of the Body* (Santa Ana, Calif.: Vision House Publishers, 1974), 154.

CHAPTER 3

1. Airhart, *BBE*, 109.
2. Stedman, *Birth of the Body*, 159.
3. Ibid., 160.
4. Jacobsen, *Acts Then and Now*, 81.
5. Lloyd John Ogilvie, *Drumbeat of Love* (Waco, Tex.: Word Books, 1976), 134-35.

CHAPTER 4

1. R. C. H. Lenski, *The Interpretation of the Acts of the Apostles* (Minneapolis: Augsburg Publishing House, 1961), 380.
2. Buttrick, *Interpreter's Bible*, 9:129.

CHAPTER 5

1. Thomas A. Carruth, *Total Prayer for Total Living* (Grand Rapids: Zondervan Publishing House, 1962), 29.

2. Stedman, *Birth of the Body,* 171.
3. Ibid.

CHAPTER 6

1. Clovis G. Chappell, *Men That Count* (New York: Harper and Brothers, 1929), 50.
2. John T. Seamands, *On Tiptoe with Love* (Kansas City: Beacon Hill Press of Kansas City, 1971), 89-90.

CHAPTER 7

1. William Barclay, *The Acts of the Apostles,* The Daily Study Bible (Philadelphia: Westminster Press, 1953), 91-92.
2. William P. Barker, *They Stood Boldly* (Westwood, N.J.: Fleming H. Revell Co., 1967), 86-87.
3. W. A. Criswell, *The Baptism, Filling, and Gifts of the Holy Spirit* (Grand Rapids: Zondervan Publishing House, 1973), 14.
4. Seamands, *On Tiptoe with Love,* 51.
5. William Greathouse, *The Fullness of the Spirit* (Kansas City: Beacon Hill Press, 1958), 82-83.

CHAPTER 8

1. Barker, *They Stood Boldly,* 92.
2. Ibid., 93.
3. Stedman, *Birth of the Body,* 185-86.
4. Eleanor B. Beakey, "Room in the Pew," *Guideposts,* Sept., 1976.
5. Jerry Cook, *Love, Acceptance, and Forgiveness* (Glendale, Calif.: Regal Books, a division of G/L Publications, 1979), 123.

CHAPTER 9

1. Airhart, *BBE,* 28.
2. Carruth, *Total Prayer for Total Living,* 28.
3. E. Stanley Jones, *How to Be a Transformed Person* (New York: Abingdon-Cokesbury Press, 1951), 313.
4. Buttrick, *Interpreter's Bible,* 9:159.
5. Charles L. Allen, *Prayer Changes Things* (Westwood, N.J.: Fleming H. Revell Co., 1964), 10.
6. Ogilvie, *Drumbeat of Love,* 160-61.
7. Ibid., 161.
8. Ibid.

Bibliography

Airhart, Arnold E. *Beacon Bible Expositions.* Vol. 5, *Acts.* Kansas City: Beacon Hill Press of Kansas City, 1977.

Alford, Henry. *The New Testament for English Readers.* Chicago: Moody Press, n.d.

Allen, Charles L. *Prayer Changes Things.* Westwood, N.J.: Fleming H. Revell Co., 1964.

Angell, C. Roy. *Shields of Brass.* Nashville: Broadman Press, 1965.

Asch, Sholem. *The Apostle.* Translated by Maurice Samuel. New York: G. P. Putnam's Sons, 1943.

Banks, Louis Albert. *Paul and His Friends.* New York: Funk and Wagnalls Co., 1898.

Barclay, William. *God's Young Church.* Philadelphia: Westminster Press, 1970.

————. *The Acts of the Apostles.* The Daily Study Bible. Philadelphia: Westminster Press, 1953.

Barker, William P. *Saints in Aprons and Overalls.* Westwood, N.J.: Fleming H. Revell Co., 1959.

————. *They Stood Boldly.* Westwood, N.J.: Fleming H. Revell Co., 1967.

Beakey, Eleanor B. "Room in the Pews." *Guideposts,* September, 1976.

Blaikie, William G. *A Manual of Bible History.* New York: Ronald Press Co., 1940.

Blair, Edward P. *The Acts and Apocalyptic Literature.* New York: Abingdon-Cokesbury Press, 1946.

Bruce, F. F. *Commentary on the Book of Acts. The New International Commentary on the New Testament.* F. F. Bruce, editor. Grand Rapids: Wm. B. Eerdmans Publishing Co., 1954.

————. *New Testament History.* Garden City, N.Y.: Doubleday and Co., 1971.

Buttrick, George Arthur, editor. *The Interpreter's Bible.* Vol. 9. New York: Abingdon Press, 1954.

Carruth, Thomas A. *Total Prayer for Total Living.* Grand Rapids: Zondervan Publishing House, 1962.

Carter, Charles W., and Earle, Ralph. *The Evangelical Commentary on the Acts of the Apostles.* Grand Rapids: Zondervan Publishing House, 1959.

Carver, Wm. Owen. *The Acts of the Apostles.* Nashville: Broadman Press, 1966.

Chadwick, Samuel. *God Listens.* Westchester, Ill.: Good News Publishers, 1973.

Chappell, Clovis G. *Men That Count.* New York: Harper and Brothers, 1929.

Clarke, Adam. *Clarke's Commentary.* Vol. 5. New York: Abingdon Press, n.d.

Cook, Jerry. *Love, Acceptance, and Forgiveness.* Glendale, Calif.: Regal Books, a division of G/L Publications, 1979.

Criswell, W. A. *The Baptism, Filling, and Gifts of the Holy Spirit.* Grand Rapids: Zondervan Publishing House, 1973.

Davidson, F., editor. *The New Bible Commentary.* Grand Rapids: Wm. B. Eerdmans Publishing Co., 1958.

Davies, G. Henton; Richardson, Allen; and Wallis, Charles L., editors. *Twentieth Century Bible Commentary.* New York: Harper and Brothers, Publishers, 1955.

DeHaan, M. R. *Pentecost and After.* Grand Rapids: Zondervan Publishing House, 1964.

Demaray, Donald E. *The Book of Acts.* Grand Rapids: Baker Book House, 1959.

Ellicott, Charles John, editor. *A Bible Commentary for English Readers.* Vol. 7. London: Cassell and Co., n.d.

Fallis, William J. *Studies in Acts.* Nashville: Broadman Press, 1949.

Gould, J. Glenn. *Healing the Hurt of Man.* Kansas City: Beacon Hill Press of Kansas City, 1971.

Greathouse, William. *The Fullness of the Spirit.* Kansas City: Beacon Hill Press, 1958.

Halley, Henry H. *Bible Handbook.* Grand Rapids: Zondervan Publishing House, 1959.

Henry, Carl F. H., editor. *The Biblical Expositor.* Vol. 3. Philadelphia: A. J. Holman Co., 1960.

Henry, Matthew. *Commentary on the Whole Bible.* Edited by Leslie F. Church. Grand Rapids: Zondervan Publishing House, 1961.

Jacobsen, Henry. *The Acts Then and Now.* Wheaton, Ill.: Scripture Press Publications, 1973.

Kingsley, Florence Morse. *Paul: A Herald of the Cross.* Philadelphia: Henry Altemus, 1898.

Kivengere, Bishop Festo. *I Love Idi Amin.* Old Tappan, N.J.: Fleming H. Revell Co., 1977.

LaSor, William Sanford. *Church Alive.* Glendale, Calif.: G/L Publications, 1972.

————. *Great Personalities of the New Testament.* Westwood, N.J.: Fleming H. Revell Co., 1961.

Lenski, R. C. H. *The Interpretation of the Acts of the Apostles.* Minneapolis: Augsburg Publishing House, 1961.

Mayfield, Joseph H., and Earle, Ralph. *John—Acts.* Vol. 7 of *Beacon Bible Commentary.* Kansas City: Beacon Hill Press of Kansas City, 1965.

McCumber, William E. *Preaching Holiness from the Synoptic Gospels.* Kansas City: Beacon Hill Press of Kansas City, 1972.

Morgan, G. Campbell. *The Acts of the Apostles.* Westwood, N.J.: Fleming H. Revell Co., 1924.

Oates, Wayne E. *Pastoral Counseling in Social Problems: Extremism, Race, Sex, Divorce.* Philadelphia: Westminster Press, 1966.

Ogilvie, Lloyd John. *Drumbeat of Love.* Waco, Tex.: Word Books, Publishers, 1976.

Parrott, Leslie. *Perspectives in Bible Holiness.* Kansas City: Beacon Hill Press of Kansas City, 1968.

Pfeiffer, Charles F. *Baker's Bible Atlas.* Grand Rapids: Baker Book House, 1961.

Pfeiffer, Charles F., and Harrison, Everett F., editors. *The Wycliffe Bible Commentary.* Chicago: Moody Press, 1962.

Popov, Haralan. *Tortured for His Faith.* Grand Rapids: Zondervan Publishing House, 1972.

Purkiser, W. T. *Interpreting Christian Holiness.* Kansas City: Beacon Hill Press of Kansas City, 1971.

————, ed. *The Church in a Changing World.* Kansas City: Beacon Hill Press of Kansas City, 1973.

Robertson, Archibald Thomas. *Word Pictures in the New Testament.* Vol. 3. Nashville: Broadman Press, 1930.

Seamands, John T. *On Tiptoe with Love.* Kansas City: Beacon Hill Press of Kansas City, 1971.

Smith, James Roy. *God Still Speaks in the Space Age.* Kansas City: Beacon Hill Press of Kansas City, 1970.

Smith, Timothy L. "Methodists and the Wesleyan Mission: Can Nazarenes Learn from Their History?" A paper presented at the 1979 Nazarene Leaders' Conference via *Ministers Tape Club.* Kansas City: Beacon Hill Press of Kansas City, 1979 (MTC TAX-1979-13).

Spence, H. D. M., and Excell, Joseph S., editors. Vol. 1, *The Acts of the Apostles, The Pulpit Commentary.* London: Funk and Wagnalls Co., 1908.

Stedman, Ray C. *Birth of the Body*. Santa Ana, Calif.: Vision House Publishers, 1974.

Stewart, James S. *King for Ever.* Nashville: Abingdon Press, 1975.

Stirling, John F. *An Atlas Illustration of the Acts of the Apostles and the Epistles.* New York: Fleming H. Revell Co., n.d.

Stratton, John G. "He Loses a Friend—and His Religious Cool." *Los Angeles Times*, n.d.

Thomas, W. H. Griffith. *Outline Studies in the Acts of the Apostles.* Grand Rapids: Wm. B. Eerdmans Publishing Co., 1956.

Trueblood, Elton. *The Incendiary Fellowship.* New York: Harper and Row, 1967.

Unger, Merrill F. *Unger's Bible Handbook.* Chicago: Moody Press, 1967.

Vaughn, Curtis. *Acts: A Study Guide.* Grand Rapids: Zondervan Publishing House, 1974.

Wilcox, Vernon L. "Ananias and the Lord." *Herald of Holiness* magazine. Kansas City: Nazarene Publishing House, Mar. 1, 1976.

Wynkoop, Mildred Bangs. *A Theology of Love.* Kansas City: Beacon Hill Press of Kansas City, 1972.